THE GREAT SUPPRESSION

"By weaving together lesser known aspects of American history going back to the Founding, the politics of today, and real stories, Roth exposes the troubling state of American democracy. He demonstrates the vast range of tactics conservative elites are using to silence Americans' voices and skew public policy in favor of the one percent. But he also lifts up recent successes in expanding voting rights and reducing money in politics, suggesting hope for a path forward."

—**Tova Wang, author of** *The Politics of Voter Suppression:*
Defending and Expanding Americans' Right to Vote

"A riveting look at the project of putting American political democracy in a straitjacket and throwing it into the backseat for a right-wing joyride. Every page in this book screams out that it's time to take our democracy back."

—**Jamie Raskin, Maryland state senator and professor of**
constitutional law, American University

"In this astute book, Zachary Roth pulls together seemingly disparate trends in our politics—from new voter-ID laws to the super-PAC free-for-all—to present a persuasive account of what democracy looks like to the modern American right."

—**Sasha Issenberg, author of** *The Victory Lab:*
The Secret Science of Winning Campaigns

"America is less democratic than we'd like to think, and it's getting even worse—that's the inescapable takeaway of *The Great Suppression.* Zachary Roth deftly reveals how a well-organized and determined minority have used restrictive voting measures and legal challenges designed to obliterate longstanding laws and to subvert the democratic process. A jarring and important read."

—**Daniel Schulman, author of** *Sons of Wichita: How the Koch*
Brothers Became America's Most Political and Private Dynasty

"Zachary Roth exposes widespread, under-reported, and dangerous machinations to disenfranchise voters and undermine our democracy, including attempts to rig the electoral college. Thankfully, as Roth reports, the tide is turning. I urge you to read this troubling–yet hopeful–book."

—Wendell Potter, former health insurance executive
and coauthor of *Nation on the Take: How Big Money
Corrupts Our Democracy and What We Can Do About It*

"Zachary Roth has written a punchy and to-the-point book about the desperate right-wing campaign to hold on to government power by limiting democratic rights. Read this book to understand the ongoing political battles roiling our country."

—Frances Fox Piven, distinguished professor of political science
and sociology, CUNY Graduate Center, and coauthor of *Why
Americans Still Don't Vote: And Why Politicians Like It That Way*

THE GREAT SUPPRESSION

Voting Rights,
Corporate Cash, and the
Conservative Assault
on Democracy

ZACHARY ROTH

CROWN
NEW YORK

Library of Congress Cataloging-in-Publication Data
Names: Roth, Zachary.
Title: The great suppression: voting rights, corporate cash, and the
    conservative assault on democracy / Zachary Roth.
Description: First edition. | New York: Crown, 2016.
Identifiers: LCCN 2016003489 (print) | LCCN 2016013542 (ebook) |
    ISBN 9781101905760 (hardback) | ISBN 9781101905777 (paperback) |
    ISBN 9781101905784 (ebook)
Subjects: LCSH Conservatism–United States. | Democracy–United
    States. | Right-wing extremists–United States. | Voting–United States.
    | Campaign funds–United States. | Political culture–United States. |
    BISAC: POLITICAL SCIENCE / Political Ideologies / Democracy. |
    HISTORY / United States / 21st Century. | POLITICAL SCIENCE /
    Political Ideologies / Conservatism & Liberalism.
Classification: LCC JC573.2.U6 R67 2016 (print) | LCC JC573.2.U6
    (ebook) | DDc 320.520973–dc23
LC record available at http://lccn.loc.gov/2016003489

ISBN 978-1-101-90576-0
Ebook ISBN 978-1-101-90578-4

PRINTED IN THE UNITED STATES OF AMERICA

Book design by Anna Thompson
Jacket design by Tal Goretsky
Jacket photographs: (arm with saw) *PM Images/Getty Images;*
(sign) *Tim Roberts/Getty Images*

10 9 8 7 6 5 4 3 2 1

First Edition

For Cassi

Contents

THE GREAT OBAMA FREAKOUT

During his 2012 campaign for Congress, Ted Yoho appeared before a friendly Tea Party group at a church in northern Florida. A licensed veterinarian and conservative Republican, Yoho hit all the high notes of the modern right. He warned that the United States was approaching a "European-style socialism, or worse—maybe a fascism." He fulminated against foreign aid and said the United Nations "needs to go." He complained that his taxes went to support people like the young men he'd recently seen using food stamps to buy chips and Arizona Iced Tea.

Then, as things were winding down, a man at the back spoke up to lament the state's recent trend toward absentee and early voting, which, he warned, raised the threat of fraud and stolen elections. Yoho, standing at the pulpit, a large American flag pinned to the wall behind him, agreed. But the real problem with making voting easier, he ventured, wasn't the opportunity for fraud. It was something more pernicious: ignorant voters. "I can't remember which Founding Father said it," Yoho mused, "but he said the ability to vote, but vote uninformed, is as tragic or as dangerous as having a loaded gun and not knowing how to use it." He praised Republican governor Rick Scott for shortening the state's early voting period from two weeks to one and added that it should be cut further.

"It's a privilege to vote," Yoho went on, warming to his theme. "Yeah, it may be inconvenient, but you know, it's like I told people when I was growing up: to be successful is inconvenient. If not, everybody would be successful."

"I've had some radical ideas about voting, and it's probably not a good time to tell you about them," Yoho added a few moments later. "But you used to have to be a property owner to vote." The crowd applauded loudly.

Voting was certainly inconvenient for many Floridians that year, just as Yoho had hoped. With those cuts to early voting causing longer lines at the polls, some waited as long as seven hours to cast a ballot, and an estimated 200,000 gave up in frustration. Twelve years after the Florida recount fiasco, the state was again the poster child for electoral chaos.[*]

Of course, Yoho's overwhelmingly white, middle-class supporters didn't seem to have trouble getting to the polls. And his nostalgia for a time when those without means were blocked from voting didn't hurt him in his conservative district. He beat a twelve-term incumbent in the Republican primary, then easily won the general election. He now sits on the Foreign Affairs Committee, and in 2015 he briefly put himself forward as a challenger to then–House Speaker John Boehner.

———

[*] The following year, embarrassed state lawmakers would restore the early voting days.

FEW IN POSITIONS of real power are quite as candid as Yoho was that day. But the notion that certain groups of Americans should be discouraged or even barred from voting—an idea thought to have long been consigned to the trash heap of history—has quietly been making a comeback. Everywhere you turn, conservatives from Republican politicians to Fox News hosts to respected newspaper columnists are lamenting the consequences of universal suffrage, and in some cases suggesting ways around it.

Yoho's notion that uninformed voters pose a mortal danger to the republic has been an article of faith on the right at least since Barack Obama's election in 2008. Just a few weeks after that contest, the conservative journalist John Ziegler posted a video on YouTube titled "How Obama Got Elected." It featured interviews with a handful of Obama voters, in which they admitted they didn't know who people like Nancy Pelosi, Harry Reid, and Barney Frank were. It's been viewed more than three million times.

A 2012 Howard Stern segment that went viral on the right played on a similar idea. Obama voters were asked if they approved of the president's choice of Paul Ryan as his running mate, or whether they expected the United States to succeed in getting Osama bin Laden—who in fact had been killed the previous year. Then the hosts chuckled over voters' ignorance in not correcting them. Both productions reflected a sentiment that's become widespread among conservatives: that Obama's backers aren't informed enough to make wise choices. When I typed "Obama voters" into Google, the third autofill suggestion it provided was "Obama voters are ignorant," a search that produced more than 1.8 million results.

But beneath the sneering tone, the videos, like Yoho's

remarks, concealed a kind of panic that the Obama era has instilled among many on the right. Conservatives had always believed that elections work—or at least should work—a certain way: people make a sober analysis of which candidate can best govern, then vote accordingly. The masses who had turned out for Obama, though, didn't seem to act that way. In the eyes of many conservatives, we were witnessing the rise of the stupid voter. "The low-information voters are now the new kings," the radio host Rush Limbaugh fretted to his millions of listeners not long after Obama was reelected. "The morons, the people that don't pay attention."

To many on the right, the problem went further: people were voting not just out of ignorance, but with only their own narrow interests, not the country's, in mind. When Mitt Romney complained about the 47 percent of Americans who don't pay income taxes, it was his dismissal of nearly half the country as lazy and unmotivated that did the political damage. But Romney's central point was slightly different—it was about how, in his view, many Democrats approach voting.

"There are 47 percent of the people who will vote for the president no matter what," Romney said, singling out those "who are dependent upon government, who believe that they are victims, who believe the government has a responsibility to care for them, who believe they are entitled to health care, to food, to housing, to you-name-it—that that's an entitlement, and the government should give it to them." Then he repeated his key point: *"And they will vote for this president no matter what."* To Romney, the biggest problem wasn't simply that these free-loaders were forcing the rest of us to support them. It was that Obama and his backers saw politics as transactional: give me stuff, and I'll vote for you in return. Romney was expressing the fear that the votes of almost half the country had been bought.

His formulation may have been artless, but Romney's larger claim remains a central strand of the story the right tells about American politics. Rather than considering what's best for the country as a whole, the idea goes, Democratic voters—meaning primarily the poor, minorities, many young people, and, perhaps, unmarried women who are sexually active—are allowing themselves to be bribed by promises of free health care, lavish unemployment benefits, college aid, and other goodies. In short, the game is rigged. A few months earlier Romney himself bragged to supporters about how he'd told an NAACP audience that if they wanted more "free stuff" like Obamacare, they should "vote for the other guy." In a postmortem after his election defeat, he explained that he'd lost because Obama had been "very generous" toward "loyal Democratic constituencies," mentioning "free contraceptives" and "amnesty." The idea endures: asked on the campaign trail in 2015 how he'd attract black support, Jeb Bush contrasted his approach to the one Democrats supposedly use. "Our message is one of hope and aspiration," Bush said. "It isn't one of division and get in line and we'll take care of you with free stuff."

Of course, it's one thing to wring your hands that some voters approach politics this way (though few on the right get this angry about forms of government largesse—say, farm subsidies or corporate giveaways in the tax code—that benefit groups they have more in common with). And conservatives certainly aren't alone in lapsing into elitism and contempt toward the other side's supporters when they lose. After President George W. Bush's 2004 reelection, a map titled "JesusLand" went viral among liberals. It showed all of Red America, from Idaho to Florida, as one vast expanse of knuckle-dragging fundamentalism. Still, almost no one on the left responded to that defeat by questioning religious conservatives' right to vote—or by expressing doubts about the very notion of popular rule. But in a development that has been all the more striking for flying largely under the radar, the age of Obama has seen the resurfacing among conservatives of a profound skepticism about the consequences of democracy itself.

It's an ideology whose roots go back to the Founders, many of whom worried that giving too much power to ordinary people would pose a threat to what they considered core values of civilized society like respect for private property, and pave the way for anarchy, despotism, or other forms of radicalism. Democracy "soon wastes, exhausts, and murders itself," John Adams wrote. "There never was a democracy yet that did not commit suicide."

Over the centuries, the salience of this way of thinking declined as a culture of democratic rights gained strength. But the fear of the mob never entirely lost its hold among many conservatives. As late as the 1920s, a U.S. Army training manual defined democracy as a form of government that results in "demagogism" and "anarchy." William F. Buckley Jr., perhaps the most important figure in shaping modern conservatism, found in this tradition of thought a defense of Jim Crow. "It is more important for any community anywhere in the world," he wrote in 1957, "to affirm and live by civilized standards than to bow down to the demands of the numerical majority." Even the sainted Ronald Reagan expressed qualms about democracy. In a 1965 speech to Ohio Republicans delivered as he was building a national reputation as a critic of big government, Reagan approvingly cited a nineteenth-century writer's view that democracy "can only exist until the voters discover they can vote themselves largesse out of the public treasury." After that, Reagan continued, anticipating Romney's 47 percent critique, the majority "always vote for the candidate promising the most benefits . . . with the result that democracy always collapses over a loose fiscal policy, always to be followed by a dictatorship."

This distrust of democracy has also played a crucial role in shaping the right's view of the Constitution as a bulwark against majoritarian tyranny—a view espoused by everyone from fringe Tea Party activists to the most powerful institutions of the conservative movement. "The Framers founded a republic because they recognized that mob rule could be just as great a threat to liberty as the rule of a king," the Heritage Foundation, Washington's most important conservative think tank, explains on its website. "America's constitutional framework thereby seeks to protect the people from the dangers of unchecked popular democracy."

The circumstances of Obama's rise to power were tailor-made to prompt the resurfacing of these kinds of anxieties on the right. It helps to remember that the period around the 2008 election was a deeply traumatic time for many Americans. The world financial system, and with it the U.S. economy, seemed to be dangling by a thread. A discredited Republican president was spending hundreds of billions to bail out Wall Street bankers before slinking out of office. And along came a smooth-talking champion of the people promising change.

"Is the allure of a charismatic demagogue so strong that the usually sober American people are willing to risk an Obama presidency?" the wildly popular conservative radio host and author Mark Levin wrote a week or so before the election. Levin's portrayal of Obama drew on a long-standing trope of conservative thought: the fear of the rabble-rouser who uses his rhetorical gifts to hoodwink the masses into supporting dangerously radical policies. In 1878 one prominent historian argued that the hordes of newly arrived immigrant workingmen filling industrial cities shouldn't be allowed to vote—a popular view at the time—in part because their "ears are open to the promptings of every rascally agitator." Around the same time, another writer concluded that universal suffrage "establishes the way to demagogism" because the "ignorant, uncultured, or dissipated voter most willingly yields to the persuasions of one of his own class."

In one symptom of the panicked atmosphere that accompanied Obama's ascendance, bizarre conspiracy theories and apocalyptic nightmares blossomed on the fringe. The new president was going to establish FEMA concentration camps, or else he'd use the United Nations to implement a global ban on guns. Even among more mainstream conservatives, a sense of foreboding prevailed. At its root was the fear that economic turmoil and the failure of the Bush presidency had opened the door to an angry and ignorant mob bent on reshaping society. When Obama awkwardly suggested on the campaign trail that he planned to "spread the wealth around," he stoked the genuine fears of many conservatives that that was exactly what was coming.

There are plenty of reasons to believe that the president's race played into these fears. But to many on the right, the demographics of those who voted for him were just as unsettling.

Both of Obama's presidential campaigns conducted unprecedented outreach to racial minorities, the poor, and the young. These groups had traditionally been alienated from politics. But they ultimately provided Obama's staunchest support. Consider that in 2012 the president won just 39 percent of white voters. Not long ago that would have almost guaranteed his defeat. But because he won 80 percent of nonwhite voters—and crucially, those voters made up 28 percent of the electorate, a higher share than ever before—he still won reelection comfortably.

Obama's success in turning out these voters was in part thanks to new, sophisticated voter targeting technology, which made them easier to reach. But it was also the result of a genuine philosophical commitment to grassroots organizing on the part of his team. By opening hundreds of field offices in communities across the country, sometimes over a year ahead of the election, the Obama campaign succeeded in bringing millions of new voters into the process.

This was profoundly unsettling to many conservatives—much more so than if Obama had prevailed the old-fashioned way, by winning over moderate swing voters. More worrying still has been another realization: as political polarization has increased, the number of truly persuadable voters has shrunk dramatically. A poll taken in August 2012 found 81 percent of respondents saying there was no chance whatsoever that they might change their mind about who to support—far more than at the same stage in past elections. Another analysis, by the respected political scientists Alan Abramowitz and Steven Webster, found "sharp increases in party loyalty and straight ticket voting," a trend that began in 1992 and accelerated in 2008 when Obama was elected. A third, by the political scientist Corwin

Smidt, found that the number of voters who consistently floated between parties had dropped from about 15 percent in the late 1960s to about 5 percent today. In other words, Romney's idea that Obama voters are impervious to persuasion contained a kernel of truth—though it appears to apply to his side, too.

This stark divide is bad news for conservatives, because demographic changes mean they're likely to be on the short end for a long time to come. Those nonwhite voters who accounted for 28 percent of the 2012 electorate had shot up from just 13 percent in 1992. And their numbers are likely to increase further over the next few cycles, as Hispanics and Asians—both now looking like solidly Democratic blocs, at least for the next decade or so—continue flexing their muscles at the ballot box. Another left-leaning group whose numbers are on the rise has received less attention: Single women made up 23 percent of voters in 2012—up from 19 percent four years earlier—and two out of three voted for Obama. Many experts now believe these trends give Democrats a built-in advantage—though certainly not an insurmountable one—in presidential elections.

These demographic changes—not to mention the reality of stagnating wages and growing inequality—are contributing to ideological ones, too. In 1998, 45 percent of voters told Gallup the government should redistribute wealth by taxing the rich heavily, compared to 51 percent who said it shouldn't. By 2015 those numbers were essentially reversed: 52 percent said it should, while 45 percent said it shouldn't. It's young and nonwhite voters who appear to be driving the shift. A 2015 *Wall Street Journal* poll found that Americans over 35 were four points more likely to say the government is doing too much than that it's doing too little. But Americans aged eighteen to thirty-four—a group that includes a far larger share of racial minorities—by a margin of 23 points said it's doing too little. "The country at large," wrote Peter Beinart in a January 2016 cover story for *The Atlantic,* "is moving to the left."

Of course, Donald Trump's hostile takeover of the Republican Party and the bitter split it's triggered have made it harder to talk about conservatism in America as a cohesive movement. On the one hand, Trump appears to have the same qualms about full democracy as his fellow GOPers. "You've got to have real security with the voting system," he told a New Hampshire crowd in January. "This voting system is out of control." And Trump's promises to Make America Great Again simply by telling China and Mexico what's what; his unconcealed admiration for Vladimir Putin ("at least he's a leader,"); his casual endorsement of violence against protesters; and his musing about restricting freedom of the press suggest an authoritarianism that's starkly at odds with democratic values. In this sense, Trump's backers represent the last gasp of the older white population looking to hold off the demographic tide.

And yet, vicious and dangerous as it is, the Trump phenomenon undeniably represents a genuine popular uprising. And it has brought out in many leading ideological conservatives the same fear and loathing of the mob that's usually directed at the other side. "The white American underclass is in thrall to a vicious, selfish culture whose main products are misery and used heroin needles," one *National Review* cover story recently concluded, explaining Trump's appeal in the kind of language more often applied by the right to racial minorities. "Donald Trump's speeches make them feel good. So does Oxycontin." Indeed, as of late March, some party leaders are scheming to wrest the nomination away from Trump at the convention even if he's the clear choice of Republican voters—democratic legitimacy be damned. "Democracy is pretty popular," said one anti-Trump GOP official, "but it's simply not the way we do it."

For conservatives, this acceptance of being in a minority—whether nationally or, now, perhaps in their own party, too—represents a sharp turnaround from previous decades. For much of the latter half of the twentieth century, they seemed to believe, perhaps correctly, that the bulk of the country was on their side. And indeed, between 1968 and 1988, Republicans won five out of six presidential elections, losing only the 1976 contest following the Watergate scandal. During this period, they spoke in the confident language of a majority party. In 1969 Richard Nixon appealed to the "great silent majority" of Americans who weren't part of the liberal counterculture. The same year, a young Republican operative named Kevin Phillips published a book entitled *The Emerging Republican Majority*, accurately forecasting the coming age of conservative dominance. And Ronald Reagan, whatever his real feelings about democracy, campaigned and governed with a bedrock belief—supported by plenty of public opinion data—that most of the country backed his small-government agenda.

Today's conservatives have no such confidence that the people are on their side. In fact, they're beginning to perceive that they're in the minority—perhaps more glaringly than ever before. And yet this realization has brought with it another more hopeful one: being outnumbered doesn't have to mean losing.

———

EVER SINCE OBAMA'S first election victory, conservatives have been engaged in a remarkable and little-noticed project: a kind of guerrilla effort to maintain a hold on power and fight off a progressive agenda, despite more often than not being in the minority. At its core, this bold campaign has amounted to nothing less than an effort to undermine democracy.

It's been carried out by Republican politicians and operatives, conservative lawyers, and grassroots activists, working from the halls of Congress, state capitols, well-appointed law offices, and ordinary American living rooms. Not everything they've tried has come off. But taken as a whole, they've achieved a stunning turnabout. For nearly a century, the country moved, in fits and starts to be sure, toward ever-increasing political equality. Now, thanks to their work, a new era of democratic contraction beckons, in which the central promise of our system of government—that ordinary people can mobilize to create change—is increasingly at risk.

In what has been perhaps the most explicit and cynical challenge to popular rule, Republican-led states from Arizona to Wisconsin to North Carolina have imposed a host of restrictions on voting—voter ID laws, cuts to early voting, and more—that target Democratic-leaning groups: racial minorities, students, and the poor. And thanks to a concerted conservative legal campaign, the 2016 election will be the first presidential contest in over half a century conducted without the full protections of the Voting Rights Act, the most successful civil rights law in history. In some parts of the country, Ted Yoho's cramped view of voting as a privilege for those who have earned it threatens to become a reality.

Meanwhile, before the death in February 2016 of Justice

Antonin Scalia, the Supreme Court's five conservatives largely approved a bid by the Republican Party to scrap meaningful limits on money in politics, opening the floodgates to an unprecedented barrage of campaign cash from corporations and the superrich, and warping our democracy beyond recognition. In doing so, they explicitly denied the legitimacy of efforts to ensure that all Americans have an equal say in the political process.

Republicans also have rigged Washington in their favor. GOP-controlled states, with a major assist from the national party, have fixed the congressional map to entrench their party in power for years to come—meaning that even when a majority of voters have chosen Democrats to run the House, they've gotten Republicans. And in the Senate, the GOP has used every trick in the rulebook to stop even popular bills from getting an up-or-down vote. The result has been to make it all but impossible for Congress to take action even when the public wants it to. Meanwhile, in a bid to hold off an ideological shift on the Supreme Court after Scalia's death, Republicans have essentially nullified the president's constitutional power to appoint Supreme Court justices.

Less noticed has been an effort by red states—backed by an array of corporate lobby groups—to crack down on the authority of cities and counties to pass progressive laws on everything from worker pay to public health to protecting the environment. This under-the-radar assault on local democracy threatens the last place where our political system remains reasonably responsive to ordinary people.

In case all this doesn't do the trick, a well-connected group of libertarian lawyers is bringing the campaign against democracy to the courts, too, by explicitly urging judges to be less respectful of the democratic process. These new judicial activists want to return us to a world before the New Deal, when basic worker protections and government welfare programs, no matter how popular and urgently needed, were deemed unconstitutional. Their challenge to Obamacare's individual mandate came within a hair of succeeding—and they may be closer to ultimate victory than it seems.

This remarkable campaign against democracy has stymied progress on a range of urgent issues on which most Americans clearly agree. It's often said that red and blue America are deeply divided, but in fact, on many of the key challenges we face—reducing inequality, tackling climate change, and curbing gun violence chief among them—there's a surprisingly strong consensus in favor of taking decisive action. "The real issue is that in area after area, raising the minimum wage to 15 bucks an hour, the American people want it," Bernie Sanders said at a Democratic debate in January 2016. "Rebuilding our crumbling infrastructure, creating 13 million jobs, the American people want it. The pay equity for women, the American people want it. Demanding that the wealthy start paying their fair share of taxes, the American people want it." Sanders was attributing the problem to too much money in politics, but he could have broadened his indictment to the full range of devices for thwarting the popular will that Republicans have employed lately.

To fully grasp this multipronged assault on the power of the people, we need to understand that it's driven by more than partisan politics. To be sure, it's the natural instinct of any political movement to advance its agenda. Making it harder for Democrats to vote, allowing the wealthy to spend unlimited sums on campaigns, and gerrymandering the congressional map all help Republicans get elected. Stopping cities from passing worker or environmental protections pleases key industry supporters. Getting courts to limit the kind of economic regulation Congress can pass aligns with most conservatives' small-government policy preferences. And so on. Of course, Democrats are no less partisan. They oppose these moves largely because doing so serves their political or policy interests.

But that doesn't tell the whole story. Scratch beneath the surface of the arguments for voter ID laws, and you often discover a core belief, like Yoho's, that voting isn't really for everyone. Look closely at the push for more assertive judges, and you can't help but notice a striking dismissiveness, at best, about the democratic process. Examine the effort to eviscerate campaign finance laws, and you'll find a scathing contempt for the principle of political equality.

In other words, these fights aren't just isolated spats over process, or self-interested interparty skirmishes. They reflect fundamentally divergent worldviews. One sees democracy as a normative good in itself, and as crucial to any claim to political legitimacy. The other sees it as at best a method for achieving effective government, and at worst a blueprint for chaos.

That leads to a troubling conclusion: Most of us like to think that although Americans might disagree profoundly on many issues, and even on values like how to balance liberty with the common good, we all share a commitment to democracy as the way to resolve these differences. In fact, that consensus may be far more fragile than we'd like to think.

Chapter 1

BLOCK THE VOTE

The city of Beaumont, Texas, sits about thirty miles from the Louisiana border, and it feels like the place where the Gulf Coast meets the Deep South. On the streets, signs advertising Cajun specialties like boudin balls and étouffée stand next to palm trees in the swampy heat. Outside Beaumont's best hotel, a ten-foot-tall stone tablet engraved with the Ten Commandments offers a warning to business travelers who might be led into temptation. It was in nearby Jasper that white supremacists dragged a black man named James Byrd to his death behind a pickup truck in 1998. In February 2016, the night before local elections, a man was arrested after allegedly firing a shot into the crowded Beaumont campaign headquarters of a black female candidate for county sheriff, yelling "Fuck the niggers." The writer Joyce Carol Oates, who worked in the area as a young teacher in the 1960s, tweeted recently that though she'd never been to hell, she "did spend some time in Beaumont, Texas once."

Like those of many American cities, Beaumont's neighborhoods are heavily segregated, and for years after the civil rights era, its schools remained separate and unequal. But by the mid-1990s blacks had won a majority on the school board. Soon the board hired a charismatic black superintendent, Carroll Thomas, who invested in once-neglected schools, hired more black teachers, and promoted black administrators. Test scores rose, and racial tensions seemed to dissipate. In 2001 the Texas Association of School Administrators named Beaumont the school board of the year.

But by the end of the decade, rancor had returned. Many of Beaumont's white residents had grown angry over what they alleged was mismanagement and corruption on the part of district administrators, centered on a $389 million bond package that, they claimed, had become a slush fund for Thomas's friends and allies. At a public board meeting, Mike Getz, a conservative white lawyer and city councilman who led the opposition, angrily charged that the bond issue wouldn't help the schools but would "make 100 black men rich."

In 2011 Getz and his allies on the city council tried to gain control of the board. To do so, they placed on the ballot an initiative that took advantage of the once-a-decade redistricting planned for that year to change the way board members are elected—removing two of the seven geographical districts and replacing them with two "at-large" seats elected by the school district as a whole. Blacks outnumber whites in Beaumont by about 47 percent to 40 percent, and four of the seven districts were majority black. But whites vote at a higher rate—and very few vote for black candidates. That meant the move would likely reduce the number of seats held by blacks. Indeed, at-large voting schemes have for decades been a favorite tactic of conservative whites looking to hold off minority political power.

Thanks to overwhelming support from white voters, the initiative passed. But the following year the U.S. Justice Department stepped in and blocked the change, citing Section 5 of the Voting Rights Act. A response to Jim Crow laws that kept blacks from the polls, Section 5 empowered the federal government to stop any change to election rules in certain parts of the country with a history of racial discrimination, mostly the South, if the change might harm the voting power of racial minorities.

So the conservatives tried a new tack. In March 2013 three conservative-backed candidates waited until a few minutes before the deadline, then filed papers to challenge three of the four black board members—even though those members weren't up for reelection for two more years. Getz argued in court that under state law, all board members had to run again immediately after a redistricting year. And, he claimed even more audaciously that because the black members hadn't filed for reelection—after all, they hadn't thought they needed to—the challengers should be installed in office immediately.

A Texas judge agreed, in effect unseating the board members by court order without an election. But once again the Justice Department intervened under Section 5 to block the move.

That might have been the end of it—if it weren't for developments a thousand miles away in Washington, D.C. In June 2013 the Supreme Court ruled in *Shelby County v. Holder* that Section 5 of the Voting Rights Act (VRA) was no longer needed. The Court's five conservative justices decided, in the face of mountains of evidence to the contrary, that the South had made so much progress on race since the 1960s that it was unfair to single out the region for special scrutiny by continuing to fully enforce what Justice Scalia memorably called a "racial entitlement." "Our country has changed," wrote Chief Justice John Roberts.

Just like that, the feds were out of the picture in the Beaumont school board dispute. Soon afterward a court ruled that the at-large election districts favored by Beaumont's white residents should be put in place.

The story didn't end there. It turned out that there really was some corruption in the school district. Before elections under the at-large scheme could be held, two district employees pleaded guilty to embezzling more than $4 million. And an electrical contractor had been charged the previous year with overbilling the district by $1.5 million. The contractor went free after a mistrial, and no evidence surfaced that the board was aware of any malfeasance, though it appeared to have been less than aggressive in investigating. But that was enough to convince the Republicans who ran Texas's education system to declare a state of emergency in April 2014 and seize control of the board, ousting the black majority. Today a state-appointed board of managers runs Beaumont's schools.

It was a drastic step, and one Getz had been lobbying for since the previous year. I ate lunch with him at an Italian restaurant in downtown Beaumont not long after the state court, responding to *Shelby*, ruled in favor of the at-large plan. Despite that decision, Getz wasn't inclined to leave things to the whims of a popular vote, even with the favorable districts he'd maneuvered to get. Only the state stepping in, he said, could solve the problem once and for all. "That would just cut all this nonsense out," Getz said over his chicken parmesan, "and we won't have to worry about elections."

To some black Beaumonters, the triumph of that mind-set is exactly what they feared would happen when *Shelby* came down. "Things that we never thought we would have to worry about again, because of the Department of Justice and the Voting Rights Act, are now coming back for us to deal with," Gwen Ambres, a member of the board's soon-to-be-ousted black majority, told me in the midst of the fight. "And I don't know that we're going to fare too well."

Beaumont wasn't the only place in the South that took advantage of *Shelby* by quietly changing its election system to reduce black or Hispanic political power. In one egregious example, Augusta, Georgia, with an assist from Republican state lawmakers, simply moved its local elections from November to April, when turnout among black voters drops significantly because statewide elections aren't also taking place. But the real damage was done at the state level. A host of southern states seized on *Shelby* to impose voter ID laws or other restrictive measures that either had been blocked under Section 5 or almost certainly would have been.

In fact, though, *Shelby* simply added momentum to an assault on voting that was already under way and that stretched far beyond the South. In all, since 2006, twenty-one states have passed laws—voter ID measures, cuts to early voting, strict registration rules, and a host of other devices—that have made it harder for millions of Americans to cast a ballot. All these laws disproportionately affect racial minorities, the poor, or the young. Most have been justified by citing the threat of voter fraud, despite no evidence whatsoever that such fraud exists on a significant level or could be stopped by the laws at issue. Indeed, studies have found that people are more likely to be struck by lightning than to commit voter impersonation fraud.

Taken as a whole, this shocking offensive has threatened to upend the consensus on all-but-universal suffrage that was forged half a century ago—and perhaps to usher in a new chapter in the saga of American democracy. Indeed, much of the political press is still struggling to accurately describe what's happened. How, in recent years, can millions of citizens have had perhaps their most basic right so casually threatened or taken away?

Crude partisanship is a large part of the answer, of course. Republicans understand that the lower the turnout, the better they do, because voters from more marginalized communities can more easily be kept or deterred from the polls, and those voters tend to support Democrats. But it's not hard to see in the conservative assault on voting something underneath partisanship: a kind of dismissal of the importance of the individual's right to vote, or a denial that such a right really exists—well expressed in Mike Getz's desire not to have to worry about elections at all. In fact, in some cases, you can even detect versions of the centuries-old belief that the very stability of society depends on ensuring that not everyone gets a say.

"There is a deep-seated division in this society," Steven Mintz, a University of Texas history professor who has written in depth about the right to vote through history, told me, "about whether it's a bad thing if those who aren't really engaged—that is, paying taxes and so on—don't vote."

CONSERVATIVES JUST DON'T think about voting the way most other Americans do.

Liberals, even at the Founding, have seen voting straightforwardly as a right and as our foremost guarantee of equality. Central to this idea is the need to represent everyone's interests. Most people don't really believe that elections have a right answer. Instead, we think different candidates will benefit different groups of voters, and that most people can figure out which candidate is on their side: parents of young children might support a candidate who promises to invest in education, seniors might prefer the one who promises to protect Social Security, and so on. More people participating means more interests are represented, which leads to a more legitimate result and a stronger democracy.

But as the election law scholar Rick Hasen has written, many conservatives have never really bought into that way of thinking. To them, voting is much more instrumental, with the goal of making a sensible collective choice that will produce effective government and promote the common good. That's how the eighteenth-century New Englanders who gathered on village greens to vote in public conceived of what they were doing. And that means an informed, independent electorate is crucial. After all, how else can voters be expected to choose wisely? It's not hard to see how, under this logic, reducing the number of uninformed voters—or less motivated voters, or voters with less of a long-term stake in their community—isn't antidemocratic, it's civic-minded.

Indeed, many conservatives explicitly reject the idea that everyone should be encouraged to vote. For much of the twentieth century, this skepticism about universal suffrage went mostly underground, as one group after another used the language of rights and equality to gain the franchise. But it never entirely went away. And in recent years it's begun to be voiced again.

Some on the right simply reject the notion that more people voting is in itself a sign of civic health. To George Will, the *Washington Post*'s influential conservative columnist, low turnout is a sign that everything's running smoothly. When people don't vote, it's because "the stakes of politics are agreeably low because constitutional rights and other essential elements of happiness are not menaced by elections," Will wrote in 2012, perhaps not defining, say, access to health insurance as essential to happiness. Will Wilkinson, a respected libertarian writer formerly with the Cato Institute, argues that low turnout isn't just a sign of civic health, it's a cause of it. "Lower turnout sets the stage for better democracy," he has written, since "the flakiest voters—the ones least motivated to show up at the polls year in and year out—also tend to be most poorly informed."

From this mind-set, it's only a short leap to worrying more openly about the problem of low-quality voters. Perhaps we can't stop them from voting if they're determined to do so, goes the thinking, but we certainly shouldn't be encouraging it. And if the election process puts up barriers that keep these people away, so much the better. "The need to register to vote is just about the most modest restriction on ballot access I can think of, which is why it works so well as a democratic filter," *National Review*'s Daniel Foster wrote in 2015. "It improves democratic hygiene because the people who can't be bothered to register . . . are, except in unusual cases, civic idiots." Or here's George Will again, in 2010: "A small voting requirement such as registration, which calls for the individual voter's initiative, acts to filter potential voters with the weakest motivations. They are apt to invest minimal effort in civic competence."

A few prominent conservatives are willing to follow Ted Yoho to the final step: disenfranchisement. Representative Steve King of Iowa, one of Congress's most influential right-wingers, seemed to go there as he wrung his hands about government spending at a 2011 hearing. "There was a time in American history when you had to be a male property owner in order to vote," King said, anticipating Yoho. The idea, King continued, was that voters should "have some skin in the game." The problem today, he went on, is that too many voters don't pay taxes, and so "when they vote, they vote for more government benefits." A 2014 Fox News segment was blunter, asking: "Is it time to revisit a test for people to be able to vote?" Minutes later Ann Coulter got to the point: "I just think it should be a little more difficult to vote. There's nothing unconstitutional about literacy tests." Jonah Goldberg, a senior editor at *National Review* and an influential pundit on the right, has proposed making would-be voters take the same test given to those applying for citizenship. "Voting should be harder, not easier," he has written elsewhere. And Glenn Reynolds, a conservative law professor and popular blogger, responded to the antiracism protests that swept college campuses in 2015 by arguing for raising the voting age to twenty-five.

Versions of this thinking are in vogue even among more scholarly types. In his 2011 book, *The Ethics of Voting,* the libertarian law professor Jason Brennan compared uninformed voters to drunk drivers. "I've actually become more sympathetic to the idea that maybe people should be formally excluded from voting," Brennan told an interviewer.

It's easy to see this kind of rhetoric as a knee-jerk reaction to demographic trends that favor progressives. But it also represents the reemergence of a deeply rooted conservative fear—something close to an ideology—that giving full voting rights to the masses will dangerously destabilize society and usher in radical change. Throughout U.S. history, that fear has frequently acted to slow and even reverse the march of greater political equality—just as it's doing today.

———

IN THE AFTERMATH of the Revolutionary War in the 1780s, a financial crisis roiled Massachusetts. Farmers in the central and western parts of the state who had taken out loans were hit hardest as eastern businessmen called in debts and the government raised property taxes to fill its own coffers. The legislature, dominated by eastern creditors, declined to take steps to address the crisis, and a bad harvest made things worse. Finally, in 1786, a war veteran named Daniel Shays led an uprising of farmers that shut down county courthouses in Northampton, Great Barrington, Concord, and other towns where foreclosure judgments were being issued against those who couldn't pay their debts.

Around that time, John Adams, who was serving as the U.S. ambassador to Britain, received a letter from a friend about the chaos in his home state. Adams wasn't too interested in the farmers' plight, but he was alarmed by the report of disorder. "I . . . am much affected with the disagreeable state of things in the Massachusetts," he wrote not long afterward. "Mobs will never do to govern states or command armies."

Shays's Rebellion was eventually put down by government-backed troops. But it was only one manifestation of broader forces that the Revolution's egalitarian ideals had set in motion—and of the terror that these forces induced in those with the most to lose. Starting in 1776, many states had loosened rules on who could vote and hold office, made elections more frequent, and drawn more equally sized districts—with the result that a new wave of men of a lower social rank gained power. The Revolution had also weakened the social hierarchy, so that those on the bottom were less inclined to bow and scrape to their onetime superiors. The "spirit of independency was converted into equality," one shocked aristocratic Virginian complained, such that a common peasant "conceives himself, in every respect, my equal."

To men like Adams, this was deeply unnerving, because it seemed to threaten the values of order, stability, and respect for private property that they prioritized over equality. "The moment the idea is admitted into society that property is not as sacred as the laws of God," Adams wrote in 1778, "anarchy and tyranny commence."

It should come as no surprise that Adams feared democracy. James Madison did, too. "Democracies have ever been spectacles of turbulence and contention," he wrote in 1787, "have ever been found incompatible with personal security or the rights of property; and have in general been as short in their lives as they have been violent in their deaths."

Even Alexander Hamilton—the scrappy immigrant and foe of slavery whose rags-to-riches story has lately made him every Broadway-goer's favorite Founding Father—was terrified of the democratic energy that the Revolution had inspired. Hamilton's famous advocacy for a powerful national government was driven in large part by the need to guarantee the new nation's economic and military resilience. But it was also a product of his desire to rein in state governments, which were emerging as strongholds of egalitarian democracy. In his only major speech at the Constitutional Convention, Hamilton said the system should allow the "rich and the well born" to maintain their supremacy, since they would oppose radical change pushed by "the many." The goal, he said, was to "check the imprudence of democracy."

Hamilton wasn't speaking only for himself. He "had pulled

back the curtain that concealed the true thoughts of the most conservative Americans," writes the historian John Ferling. Hamilton's ideology, Ferling adds, "was an expression of the elite's over-arching desire to preserve their exalted status, and its class-biased, antidemocratic spirit . . . would remain the driving force behind much of conservative philosophy for generations to come."

It certainly was influential in shaping the debate in Philadelphia. Take the crucial question of which offices would be popularly elected. Most of the delegates thought voters should consider only the personal qualities of the prominent men who ran for office, rather than worrying about the substantive issues of the day, which were to be left to those who were elected. As a result, many held that even white male property owners weren't qualified to choose between presidential candidates, since they were unlikely to know them personally. Virginia's George Mason said that letting people elect the president would be like referring "a trial of colors to a blind man." Instead, some argued, this task should be left to state legislatures. Roger Sherman of Connecticut went further. He thought state legislatures should elect members of the House and Senate, too. The people, he said, "should have as little to do as may be about the government. They want [i.e., lack] information, and are constantly liable to be misled."

As for who should get to vote in the first place, many delegates agreed with Adams, still serving in London, who had written that voting couldn't be a right because if it were, there would be "no end of it"—that is, it would have to be extended to women and blacks, which obviously was out of the question. Even Pennsylvania's James Wilson, who argued for a popularly elected Senate and presidency, saw suffrage not as a right but as a "darling privilege of free men," one that should be extended only "as far as considerations of safety and order will permit." In the end, it was agreed—fatefully—to leave the question to the states.

And so at the outset, most states disenfranchised those without property, and the rest required that voters be taxpayers. (Vermont was the first state to have neither qualification when it joined the union in 1791.) But if the U.S. system of government was a long way from democratic at first, it got much more so in the first half of the new century. As part of a broader egalitarian trend, states loosened suffrage restrictions, in many cases enfranchising all white males and even sometimes letting noncitizens vote.

It wasn't long before the backlash arrived—one that centered on a very specific fear of urban voters. Many of the Founders had believed that the American experiment in self-governance would work only as long as the United States remained a society of yeoman farmers. If it became predominantly urban, as western Europe had, corruption would inevitably set in. Soon many conservatives began to worry that that was just what was happening. New York City "is rapidly swelling into the unwieldy population, and with the burdensome pauperism, of a European metropolis," James Kent, a staunchly conservative New York judge, lamented at his state's 1821 convention, reflecting a common view among his peers. "Universal suffrage jeopardizes property, and puts it into the power of the poor and the profligate to control the affluent," Kent went on. "This democratic principle cannot be contemplated without terror."

What really helped translate these fears into policy was

the flood of new immigrants into big cities that started in the 1830s. In 1840 New York's Whigs imposed a voter registration law that applied only to New York City, where poor Irish voters, who overwhelmingly backed Democrats, were strongest. Other states began floating proposals to increase the number of years that naturalized citizens had to wait before voting, as well as to impose literacy or other educational tests. But it wasn't until Reconstruction made the issue of black suffrage unavoidable that this clash of ideologies found itself at the very center of the national debate.

THE FIFTEENTH AMENDMENT to the Constitution, passed by Congress in February 1869, reads as follows: "The right of citizens of the United States to vote shall not be denied or abridged by the United States or by any state on account of race, color, or previous condition of servitude. The Congress shall have power to enforce this article by appropriate legislation."

But as the historian Alexander Keyssar details in *The Right to Vote: The Contested History of Democracy in the United States,* the most comprehensive study yet of suffrage restrictions in America, Congress came close to passing a very different and much broader amendment—one that might have had more success at protecting voting rights, and not only for blacks, over the ensuing century. It was offered by Senator Henry Wilson, a Massachusetts Republican, and rather than focusing solely on race, it prohibited almost any form of discrimination in voting, and came close to affirming a positive right to vote. Supporters of the Wilson amendment argued that an approach confined to race was inadequate, because, as Senator Oliver Morton of

Indiana put it, it would send the message to states that "while you shall not disfranchise a man on account of color, you may disfranchise him because he has not got property."

Morton had put his finger on the key issue. Many lawmakers who were willing to accept black voting rights were a long way from signing on to any kind of broad right to vote. In the end, a conference committee approved the narrower amendment that ultimately was ratified by the states. A disappointed Wilson described it as "lame and halting." Morton called it "half a loaf."

The failure of the Wilson amendment underscored the reality that even at a moment when America's democratic ideals seemed to be at their most ascendant, many of those in power retained serious qualms about their implications. It had other practical effects, too, just as Morton had feared. In the South, Democrats used literacy tests, polls taxes, the white primary, and a host of other devices to keep blacks from the polls for another century. Northern Republicans used their own schemes, including English-language and religious tests, to disenfranchise millions of immigrants from southern and eastern Europe.

Often this retreat from democracy was driven by the same kind of demographic change we're seeing today. In the five decades or so after the end of the Civil War, over 27 million immigrants—many of them Italians, Poles, and Jews with starkly different customs and values—entered a country whose total population by 1914 was 100 million. And so the idea began to take hold that democracy had worked fine when Americans were more homogenous. But no longer. "A New England village of the olden time" could be "safely and well governed by the votes of every man," the country's most eminent historian, Francis Parkman, wrote in an 1878 essay entitled "The Failure of

Universal Suffrage." But it was a different story now that those villages had grown into cities with "tenement-houses" and "restless workmen, foreigners for the most part." For these people, Parkman wrote, "the public good is nothing and their own most trivial interests everything." Under such conditions, "universal suffrage becomes a questionable blessing." For Parkman, the critical point was that the views of the new urban masses simply lay outside that same American consensus that John Adams had wanted to protect: "They want equality more than they want liberty."

This broad retreat from democracy for a time set back the cause of women's suffrage, too. "The opposition [to women's suffrage] today seems not so much against *women* as against any more voters at all," the historian Mary Jo Adams wrote in 1898 (emphasis hers). "Suffrage is not an 'inalienable right' of the citizen, of the taxpayer or of anybody else. It exists for the good of the State and whatever is for its best interests is right."

By the time the Nineteenth Amendment finally gave women the right to vote in 1920, this era of democratic contraction had largely come to a close, thanks in part to the surging Progressive movement. The Second World War and its aftermath pushed things in the same expansive direction: southern blacks had served bravely to defeat Hitler and Mussolini, and later, denunciations of Russia's one-party system rang hollow as long as America refused to get its own democratic house in order. And so, in 1961, after over half a decade of high-profile activism, the federal Commission on Civil Rights (CCR) concluded that a new law was needed to guarantee black voting rights. But like Henry Wilson and Oliver Morton nearly a century earlier, the panel wanted to go further. It urged Congress to ban all voter qualifications other than age, felony convictions, or residency, and to pass legislation giving the right to vote to all citizens.

But just as in 1869, there was opposition to this broader approach, even from those who claimed to have no problem with black people voting. In a dissent to the CCR's recommendation, the commission's vice-chair, Robert Storey, the dean of Southern Methodist Law School, wrote that while racial and religious discrimination in voting should be banned, a universal right to vote went too far. "Many States disqualify paupers supported by municipal or county officials on the theory that these people are too easily exploitable by such officials for their own purposes," Storey wrote. "The security and purity of the ballot can be destroyed by permitting illiterates to vote. And as the English language is still the official language of the United States"—in fact, the United States has never had an official language—"there is good justification for States requiring that voters have at least a rudimentary knowledge of this language."

Ultimately, Storey prevailed. Rather than clearly affirming a fundamental right to vote, the Voting Rights Act of 1965 gave Congress the power to enforce the Fourteenth and Fifteenth Amendments by declaring that no one could be barred from voting on account of race. To be clear, the bill's sponsors had good reason to take this "negative" approach: It was the urgent cause of African-American political equality, not abstract universalism, that drove Congress and President Lyndon Johnson to act. At least over the next decade, the law was remarkably successful, finally turning millions of black southerners into full citizens and helping to end American apartheid. And in fact the poll taxes, literacy tests, and language requirements that Storey wanted to hold on to were gradually abolished over the next decade, leaving only age requirements, felony status, and residency as formal barriers to the franchise. Still, the law's exclusive focus on racial discrimination underscored the stubborn reality that, as in the century before, racist opposition to black voting rights was in some ways easier to overcome than age-old ambivalence about an expansive approach to democracy.

Not that the VRA settled the race issue, either. Its passage spurred a conservative countermovement that has worked steadily over the last five decades to narrow the scope of the law and weaken its enforcement. *Shelby County* is its crowning achievement—so far. But as Storey's reservations suggest, just as the VRA didn't end the debate over racial bias in voting, neither did it establish a real ideological consensus about universal suffrage. Indeed, in some corners, the advances of the civil rights era set off a new round of hand-wringing.

In 1975 Samuel Huntington, a prominent conservative academic and the cofounder of *Foreign Policy* magazine, produced a report on the "crisis of democracy" in the United States for the Trilateral Commission, a group of elites from the United States, western Europe, and Japan who were alarmed by diminishing public confidence in government. Huntington blamed the problem on an "excess of democracy" embodied by the popular movements of the 1960s, which he thought raised the threat of disorder and chaos. Ideally, Huntington suggested, it would be best for everyone if previously disfavored groups could go back to being disfavored. "In the past, every democratic society has had a marginal population, of greater or lesser size, which has not actively participated in politics," he wrote. "In itself, this marginality on the part of some groups is inherently undemocratic," he conceded. But that was in fact a good thing because "it has also been one of the factors which has enabled democracy to function effectively."

Huntington, who would go on to serve as an adviser to South Africa's apartheid government, acknowledged that this was unlikely, at least in the United States—blacks weren't going to return to the back of the bus. Still, we could at least vow to go no further. "We have come to recognize that there are potentially desirable limits to economic growth," he concluded. "There are also potentially desirable limits to the indefinite extension of political democracy."

Huntington's fears proved mostly unfounded. The democratic awakening of the 1960s and early '70s receded during the Carter and Reagan eras. By the 1980s, politics was again something for people (mostly middle- and upper-middle-class people) to tune in to at election time, or not. Turnout for the 1988 presidential election dropped to its lowest level since Coolidge. In response, Congress in 1993 considered a bill to make registering to vote much easier—especially for the poor, whose registration rates were particularly low—by requiring states to offer registration opportunities at the DMV and social service agencies.

The debate over the measure, known informally as "Motor Voter," was at times hard to distinguish from the arguments that had played out over the previous two centuries. "Who wins under this bill?" asked an outraged Representative Spencer Bachus, a young Republican from Birmingham, Alabama. "Well, Motor Voter, with its mandatory registration of welfare and entitlement recipients, will result in the registration of millions of welfare recipients, illegal aliens, and taxpayer funded entitlement recipients. They'll win."

With Democrats controlling Washington, Bachus's arguments failed to carry the day. And after going into effect in 1996, Motor Voter largely succeeded in boosting access to voter registration, despite the constant need to use the threat of lawsuits to get states to comply.[*]

Indeed, to some, the law may have been too successful. In Virginia, the number of registered voters ballooned by nearly 23 percent between 1995 and 1998, an increase not seen for at least two decades. The following year Jim Gilmore, the state's Republican governor, had an idea: a pilot program that, for the first time, would require voters in certain parts of the state to show an ID.

CATHERINE OVERTON MOVED from Las Vegas to Dallas in the summer of 2014 and soon registered to vote. But when she went to the polls for the midterm elections that fall, she was turned away by a poll worker who told her, "If you've been here long enough to get a voter registration card, you've been here long enough to get ID." Overton didn't know that Texas requires a photo ID to vote, and as a senior citizen who didn't drive, she didn't have one anyway.

The experience reminded Overton, who is black, of trying to cast a ballot in her native Mississippi under Jim Crow. "It

---

[*] Republicans have never come around to it, of course. A draft of the 2014 Texas GOP platform called for its repeal. And when conservatives learned that, thanks to the law, people would get the chance to register to vote when they signed up for Obamacare, it was as if their worst nightmares had been made flesh. "What do you think is really going on?" Rush Limbaugh asked his millions of listeners in 2013. "Voter registration! There is obviously massive Democrat voter registration going on at these exchanges."

brought it all back," she told me. "I'm seventy years old. I've been discriminated against my whole life."

What happened to Overton that day was the culmination of a determined conservative campaign against voting that was years in the making. In Texas, it started in earnest around 2006, when Attorney General Greg Abbott, today the state's governor, announced a $1.5 million effort to root out and prosecute voter fraud, calling it an "epidemic." But what Texas Republicans were really worried about was legitimate voters. The Lone Star State's soaring Hispanic population is projected to help turn Texas from red to purple, and perhaps blue, within the next few decades. The GOP has been working to hold off that day for as long as possible. And a voter ID law was a key part of the plan. After two failed attempts, Republican lawmakers finally rammed it through in 2011, using a sequence of rare parliamentary maneuvers to make their bill harder to block or amend.

It wasn't hard to figure out who the law targeted. Handgun licenses were included on the short list of acceptable forms of photo ID, but not student IDs. Out-of-state driver's licenses weren't accepted, either—another hurdle for many students and for minorities, who move more than whites. Nor did Texas make much effort to get its voter IDs—created for those who lacked any other form of acceptable ID—to the hundreds of thousands of registered voters who needed them. Over a quarter of the state's counties didn't have a single ID-issuing office, meaning some Texans had to travel 120 miles or more to get one. Even if they could make the trip, they'd likely need to bring a copy of their birth certificate to prove their identity. Those who didn't have one would need to order it, which would cost as much as $23. Those born out of state, of course, might have to pay more. An elderly African-American woman named Sammie Louise Bates later testified that on a monthly income of $321, she simply couldn't afford the $42 charged by her native Mississippi. "I had to put the $42 where it would do the most good," Bates said. "We couldn't eat the birth certificate." Little wonder that fourteen months after Texas started offering IDs, just 279 people had obtained them. And though the law was said to be needed to combat an epidemic of voter fraud, the state could point to just two successful prosecutions for in-person voter impersonation—the only kind of fraud the new rules might have stopped—since 2000, during which time 20 million votes had been cast.

The law's path through the legal system had been winding. Finding that it discriminated against blacks and Hispanics, a federal court blocked it in 2012 under Section 5 of the Voting Rights Act. But within hours of the Supreme Court's ruling in *Shelby County*, Abbott announced triumphantly that the ID law was back in effect. The following year, in a scathing ruling, Judge Nelva Gonzales Ramos blocked it a second time under a different part of the VRA. She wrote that Texas had passed the law in part *because of*, rather than in spite of, its impact on minorities, and she ruled it an unconstitutional poll tax in the tradition of the state's long and shameful history of suppressing poor and minority voters. "The poor should not be denied the right to vote because they have 'chosen' to spend their money to feed their family, instead of spending it to obtain" a voter ID, Gonzales Ramos wrote. But after Texas appealed, the Supreme Court stepped in again, deciding that the law should stay in effect for the 2014 midterms while the courts were hashing things out. As a result, it may have helped swing Texas's only competitive congressional race to the GOP. The law remains in force today.

It's impossible to say how many people, like Catherine Overton, were disenfranchised by the ID law in that election—though news reports turned up plenty. The district court found that around 608,000 registered voters—disproportionately minorities, and representing about 4.5 percent of all Texas voters—lacked the ID required to vote.

IN ITS ORIGINS as a response to fears about the growing power of minority voters; in the way it unquestionably hits blacks, Hispanics, students, and the poor hardest; in Texas's lackluster efforts to ensure that people have what they need to vote; in the state's utter failure to point to evidence of the kind of fraud it might prevent; in its reliance for survival on the Supreme Court's weakening of the Voting Rights Act—in all these ways, Texas's ID law typifies the wave of voter suppression schemes imposed over the last decade by Republicans from Arizona to North Carolina, Florida to Wisconsin. But the roots of this campaign go back even further.

The Florida recount of 2000 brought home to both parties that control of the White House could hinge on how ballots are cast and counted—kicking off our modern era of fights over voting access. Yet there likely would have been no recount at all if it weren't for the state's felon disenfranchisement law, a remnant of Jim Crow, which offered a reminder that if voting is a right, it's one that can easily be forfeited. According to the sociologists Jeff Manza and Christopher Uggen, who have looked closely at the impact of felon disenfranchisement laws, Al Gore "would certainly have carried the state, and the election," were it not for Florida's voting ban. And they didn't even consider that twelve thousand people were wrongly purged from voter rolls after incorrectly being named felons. Further, the Supreme Court's opinion ordering a stop to the recount and handing the election to George W. Bush, though narrowly written, was facilitated by the lack of a constitutional guarantee of a right to vote. "The individual citizen has no federal constitutional right to vote for electors for the President of the United States," the justices noted casually. Put simply, things couldn't have transpired as they did in Florida if the right to vote were as broadly accepted as we like to think it is.

And so, over the course of Bush's presidency, the first phase of the assault on voting began: an effort by Republican operatives and elected officials to stoke fear over voter fraud. Soon Karl Rove and his allies were pressuring federal prosecutors to bring voter fraud cases—and firing at least one when he declined, saying the evidence wasn't strong enough. A mysterious Washington organization set up by GOP strategists raised the alarm about illegal voting, then disappeared, never to be heard from again. Soon a handful of intrepid red states, including Georgia, Tennessee, and Indiana, passed voter ID laws. By the fall of 2008, the party's presidential nominee, John McCain, was seizing on a deceptively edited undercover video to accuse ACORN, which worked to register low-income voters, of a plot to steal the election. And to many on the right, Obama's victory that year seemed to confirm their fears. Over half of Republican respondents to a 2009 poll said ACORN stole the election for him.

The groundwork had been laid. And after Republicans, boosted by the Tea Party, gained control of a slew of state legislatures in 2010, the floodgates opened. Wisconsin, Kansas, South Carolina, Alabama, Mississippi, and Pennsylvania joined Texas in passing their own ID laws. (Pennsylvania's would be overturned by a state judge the following year, and the southern states' laws were held up or softened thanks to Section 5.) Florida cracked down on voter registration, even targeting good-government groups like the League of Women Voters that conducted registration drives. In Kansas, a new law pushed by the state's top elections official, Kris Kobach, a former Republican Party operative and anti-immigration zealot, required that people registering to vote show proof of citizenship—even though there were almost no cases of noncitizens voting in the state. The law made it all but impossible to conduct registration drives in public places, since few people think to bring their passport, if they have one, to the mall. And in 2014 it would disenfranchise as many as 24,000 people whose registration applications went unprocessed because they hadn't provided the required proof.

Shelby County would give added momentum to this wave of voter suppression. Like Texas, Alabama waited just a few hours after the ruling to announce that its ID law, which it hadn't even tried to get approved by the federal government, would now go into effect. North Carolina Republicans were slower off the mark. They waited a month before passing perhaps the most restrictive voting law in the country, a sweeping measure that included an ID requirement, cuts to early voting, the elimination of same-day voter registration, and a ban on voters casting ballots outside their own precinct, as had previously been allowed. "Yes, voting is a right," one Republican sponsor of the bill allowed, "but we also have a responsibility to do it intelligently." One study estimated that the North Carolina law disenfranchised more than thirty thousand would-be voters—disproportionately minorities—in the 2014 midterms.

Ohio wasn't directly affected by *Shelby*, but it took massive steps backward, too. After the 2004 election—in which all-day lines kept as many as 100,000 or more from the polls—the state took action, expanding early voting opportunities and creating a week in which people can register and vote on the same day. But many Republicans argue that letting people vote early produces a less-informed electorate. As Christian Adams, a former Bush administration lawyer and a leading conservative voice on voting, has written, "Early voting means stubborn voters will make uninformed decisions prematurely. Voting even one week early produces less-informed voters and dumbs down the electorate." And so, after it gained full control of Ohio's government starting in 2011, the GOP imposed a series of measures that seemed deliberately designed to revive the insanely long lines of 2004. Republicans cut evening voting hours and ended weekend voting, threatening the "Souls to the Polls" drives that many black churches had run. They reduced the minimum number of voting machines counties must have on hand. And they made it harder to get an absentee ballot. Some of those moves would be reversed after voting rights groups sued. But with Ohio again shaping up to be the single most pivotal presidential swing state in the country, it looks more likely to repeat the fiasco of 2004 than the success of 2008.

Of course, that's at least partly by design. As the last two centuries plus have taught us, not everyone sees easy access to voting as a good thing. "I think voting is a privilege that people should make more of an effort to exercise," one Republican official in Ohio said in 2015, explaining why he opposed a proposal to allow voters to register online. "That's why I think we should make it hard for people to vote, not easy."

Chapter 2

THE PLATINUM AGE

One October day in 1990 an Arizona state lawmaker named Bobby Raymond walked into the Phoenix office of J. Anthony Vincent, a Nevada businessman. Raymond, a Democrat, listened as Vincent pitched him on the benefits of allowing casino gambling in Arizona and asked whether Raymond might be able to bring any of his colleagues along on the idea. Eventually, though, Raymond lost patience. "Understand where I'm coming from," he said. "I don't give a fuck about issues. . . . I do deals," and added: "You give me what I want, I give you what you want."

Raymond's meaning was clear. So clear, in fact, that as the meeting drew to a close, Vincent gave him $10,000. That seemed to set off alarm bells. "You got a camera in here taping all this?" Raymond asked, looking around. Still, he took the cash.

Big mistake. It turned out that the man wasn't actually J. Anthony Vincent. He was a convicted con artist named Joseph Stedino who was working undercover for local law enforcement. And yes, he did have a camera in his office, whose footage would force Raymond to plead guilty to five felony counts the following year. That operation was just one piece of a broad thirteen-month anticorruption sting that would lead to criminal indictments against twenty-one people, including six other members of the Arizona legislature. "I'm trying to position myself [so] that I can live the good life and have more money," another lawmaker told Stedino. The chair of the House Judiciary Committee left a meeting with $55,000 stuffed into a gym bag. Nearly 10 percent of the legislature ultimately was implicated in the scheme, and several legislators went on to serve time in prison.

The sprawling scandal, known to press and prosecutors as AzScam, resonated in a state that had already earned a reputation for pay-to-play politics. A year earlier both of Arizona's U.S. senators had been accused of improperly intervening to prop up a bank owned by a major contributor. And the year before *that* the state's governor was indicted for perjury and forced from office over a shady campaign loan of $350,000 from a supporter. In response to AzScam, Arizona quickly passed a round of laws that imposed more stringent restrictions on lobbying. But by the mid-1990s a series of investigative reports in the *Arizona Republic*—"Lobbyists Bearing Gifts Solidify Grip on Capitol," one 1996 story declared—made clear that professional influence peddlers continued to routinely use campaign contributions and other favors to gain sway. As lawyers for the state later put it, "A seamless interplay between fundraising and lawmaking cast a web of perceived corruption over the Arizona capitol."

In 1998 Arizonans took decisive action. Voters passed, by ballot initiative, the Citizens Clean Elections Act, which established a voluntary system of public financing for campaigns. Qualified candidates would receive an initial grant of public money, plus additional "matching funds" if their opponent spent more than they did, or if an outside group spent money against them. The law meant politicians, crooked or not, had less incentive to rely on contributions from moneyed interests and to do their bidding in return.

Things worked well for nearly a decade. By 2008 two-thirds of all primary and general election candidates chose to participate in the system, and Arizona's public financing regime was becoming a model for other states and cities. During that time Connecticut, Florida, Maine, Minnesota, and North Carolina would adopt similar systems. Though some were blocked by courts, public financing was emerging as perhaps the most promising path for curbing the influence of big money in elections as the Obama era dawned.

But in 2008 a conservative Arizona political group, along with three privately funded candidates for office, challenged the law's matching funds provision. They made what might have sounded like a far-fetched claim: that the law forced them to cut back on their own spending to avoid triggering the additional funds for their opponent, and thus it unfairly restricted speech. Three years later, in *Arizona Free Enterprise Club v. Bennett,* the U.S. Supreme Court's five conservative justices agreed, striking down the matching funds provision. Though the justices left the rest of the law intact, the ruling made public financing programs in Arizona and several other states much less appealing, since candidates who took public money were now at risk of being outspent by privately funded opponents. Not surprisingly, the participation rate fell off almost immediately.

As noteworthy as the practical impact of the decision was its reasoning, which relied on, and reinforced, a stark anti-egalitarianism that has quietly been central to the successful conservative campaign to loosen limits on money in politics. Thirty-five years earlier, in *Buckley v. Valeo*, the Court had held that preventing corruption is the only permissible rationale for laws that limit political money, meaning the goal of ensuring rough political equality was forbidden. Since then the Court had at times seemed open to at least adopting a broader definition of the kind of corruption that campaign finance laws might aim to combat. But in the Arizona case, Chief Justice Roberts slammed that door shut.

Roberts gave over much of his opinion to an Inspector Javert–like search for evidence that the drafters of the law had been trying, in violation of *Buckley*, to give each candidate a fair shot. "'Leveling the playing field' can sound like a good thing," Roberts wrote. "But in a democracy, campaigning for office is not a game. It is a critically important form of speech." Indeed, Roberts appeared to take the ban on creating equality even further than *Buckley* had: as Justice Elena Kagan noted in her dissent, the Arizona law was clearly aimed both at curbing corruption *and* at leveling the playing field. That meant that in striking down matching funds, Roberts was taking the unprecedented stance that any effort to create equality was so strictly forbidden that it was enough *in itself* to disqualify a law even when it was only one of multiple rationales.

A year earlier the Court had wholeheartedly signed on to an equally troubling premise—one that has played an even larger role in giving the wealthy more influence. In the *Citizens United* case, it embraced an expansive definition of free speech that effectively transformed the First Amendment from a protector of oppressed minorities, as most of us have long seen it, to an enabler of politically engaged billionaires.

The result of these two far-reaching holdings and several other similar ones over the last few years has been to eviscerate existing campaign finance laws, ushering in a flood of political money that threatens to warp American democracy beyond recognition. But this didn't happen out of thin air. Rather, it's the culmination of another long-running and determined conservative campaign. Like the crusade to restrict voting rights, it's been driven both by partisanship and by something more deeply rooted: a core ideology that believes it's not just acceptable for corporations and the superwealthy to have an outsize say in our elections—it's actually better that way.

IN 1971 RALPH WINTER, a conservative professor at Yale Law School, wrote a paper for a publication of the American Enterprise Institute, one of the growing crop of political think tanks that were actively spreading the right's ideas in Washington. It was clear that restrictions on political money were coming: Republicans had outspent Democrats by more than two to one in the 1968 presidential race, and in 1970 President Richard Nixon had had to veto a popular bill passed by Congress that limited spending on television ads. Winter wanted to get out ahead of the coming regulations by fashioning a principled legal argument against them. To do so, he made the novel case that political spending is a form of constitutionally protected speech. "A limit on what a candidate may spend is a limit on his political speech," Winter wrote. Therefore, he warned, campaign finance regulation "raises the most serious kinds of questions about the maintenance of the open political process contemplated by the First Amendment."

The First Amendment had until then mostly been used to protect unpopular and relatively powerless groups like religious minorities and communists. Now, Winter frankly acknowledged, he was proposing to use it to defend the right of the wealthy and powerful to spend as much money as they wanted to influence elections. "We are often exhorted to show care in protecting the liberties of groups on the periphery of the process lest infringement of their rights spread to the mainstream," Winter slyly wrote. "Surely it is also that infringement in the mainstream must soon affect rights on the periphery."

The argument was ingenious, because it offered a lofty-sounding way to defend the idea that it was okay for the rich to have more political influence than other people, a notion that until then had consistently been rejected as blatantly anti-democratic. Such inequality may or may not be unfortunate, went the new line, but it's the price we pay for free speech. And what's more American than free speech?

But beneath the free speech argument, there has always been a more pragmatic one. A long tradition of conservative thought holds that granting powerful corporations an outsize role in government would broadly benefit society—just as richer or better-informed citizens might deserve more voting power than their social inferiors.

Until the late nineteenth century, money in politics wasn't really an issue because campaigns relied largely on volunteer manpower, which they got from government and party employees appointed through a patronage system. But by the 1880s that arrangement was breaking down. In 1883 Congress passed a law to create a more professional and less politicized civil service, including banning the political contributions that the parties required of government workers. In any case, with the rise of the mass media, getting out the vote was becoming less labor-intensive, meaning money, not manpower, was what campaigns needed most. Meanwhile, massive Gilded Age corporations were beginning to flex their muscles in the political sphere, and savvy political operatives soon realized that they could offer an alternative source of funding to replace the old patronage system.

The 1896 presidential election was the turning point. Democrat William Jennings Bryan's unapologetic populism terrified the powerful banking industry, and Mark Hanna, the shrewd campaign manager for Republican William McKinley, took advantage by raising an estimated $3 million from New York donors. ("There are two things that are important in politics," Hanna is said to have declared the previous year. "The first is money, and I can't remember what the second one is.") McKinley's total haul, an estimated $3.5 million, set a record that would stand for four decades—until another Democratic populist, Franklin Roosevelt, scared Wall Street again. McKinley himself stayed home in Canton, Ohio, throughout the campaign, delivering speeches from his front porch to supporters, while Bryan, a powerful orator, embarked on an unprecedented cross-country whistle-stop tour. But Hanna used the money he'd raised to flood voters with mailers, brochures, printed speeches, and other pro-McKinley messages—enough to ensure a narrow Republican victory.

By then concern about the impact of corporate money in politics was already leading to efforts to limit it. Among the first was an amendment proposed at New York State's 1894 constitutional convention, which would have barred corporations from contributing to campaigns. The basic logic of the measure was straightforward and little different from that of many of today's campaign finance laws. It was designed, its sponsor Elihu Root told the delegates, "to prevent the great moneyed corporations of the country from furnishing the money with which to elect members of the Legislature of this State in order that these members of the Legislature may vote to protect the corporations." The goal, Root continued, was to combat "a constantly growing evil in our political affairs, which has, in my judgment, done more to shake the confidence of the plain people of small means of this country in our political institutions than any other practice which has ever obtained since the foundation of our government."

Root's measure was ultimately tabled. And in the ensuing years, conservatives began developing a positive argument for why corporations actually *should* play a central role in politics and government: essentially, because business leaders, like those elite elected officials envisioned by Hamilton and Madison, were better than ordinary Americans. In 1898 John Burgess, a Columbia University political science professor, defined corporations as "a group of human beings, usually belonging to the best class of citizens . . . and endowed with certain privileges and obligations." Burgess saw corporations as a way for citizens to band together and exercise popular sovereignty—by which he mostly seems to have meant defending private property rights. He called the corporation "as natural a defender of property against the encroachments of the government as is the individual man himself, and on account of its power . . . a far more effective defender." George Perkins, a partner at J.P. Morgan and a top fund-raiser for President Theodore Roosevelt, expanded on Burgess's argument a decade later. In a lecture at Columbia, Perkins assured his listeners that corporations recognized their responsibilities to the public. As a result, he argued, government regulators should come from the ranks of the industries they oversee, since a railroad executive, for instance, would act "in the best interests of the public and the railroad at one and the same time. Thus the businessman would merge into the public official . . . and would act the part of statesman."*

But the public didn't seem to buy these arguments. Soon after the turn of the century, concern about the corrupting influence of money in politics reached a critical mass, thanks to a series of scandals in which business leaders were found to have used corporate funds to make political contributions to the presidential campaigns of McKinley and Roosevelt. The core premise of those pushing for reform appears to have been widely accepted at the time: that effective democracy requires a reasonably level playing field. As the *New-York Tribune* editorialized in 1905, "[Corporate] stockholders, no matter how wise or how rich, should be forced to exercise their political influence as individuals on an equality with other men. That is the basic principle of democracy." Over the next few years, sweeping bipartisan majorities in Congress passed a series of measures that barred corporations from contributing to campaigns, imposed disclosure requirements, and set limits on how much campaigns

---

* Modern-day conservatives often make the same case. It made sense that many of the people President George W. Bush named to top environmental posts came from the industries they were charged with regulating, one mining industry lobbyist said, because "you've got to get the people who understand the issues."

and political committees could spend. Together these basic reforms represented the first wave of efforts to reduce the influence of political money.

The reforms certainly didn't put an end to government corruption. In the early 1920s President Warren Harding's interior secretary, Albert B. Fall, was found to have taken bribes from oil companies in exchange for leasing them the rights to reserves at Teapot Dome in Wyoming—perhaps the biggest political scandal until Watergate. Still, they do appear to have helped usher in a strikingly long period in which the parties broadened their financial bases and made themselves somewhat less reliant on massive donations from big business and its representatives. This was as much thanks to an unspoken consensus that raking in corporate contributions was simply *wrong*—and perhaps likely to backfire by generating public outrage—as it was to the letter of the law. But that consensus was important: it meant that ensuring political equality and keeping corporate money out of politics were broadly seen as legitimate and important goals.

Still, the pro-corporate ideology articulated by Burgess and Perkins never went away entirely. After President Harry Truman seized the steel mills in 1952 in response to labor unrest, John Jessup, the editor of *Fortune* magazine, argued in a speech at Harvard Business School that only corporations could now defend liberty from a rapacious government. They were suited to "this important political office," Jessup said, in part because they reflected the virtues of "efficiency, thrift, and honesty." Indeed, he went on, there was no need for the government-run social safety net that was then taking shape, because corporations already were becoming "a sort of welfare community" by providing health insurance and pensions.

Burgess, Perkins, and Jessup all believed, writes the historian Robert Mutch, that "the country would be much better governed if corporations could be made into a kind of fourth branch of government." By the early 1970s, Winter and his allies were making a slightly different, and on its face more cautious, argument: that corporations should have a political voice as citizens. "A key element of the old corporatist argument remains though," Mutch adds. "A distrust of democracy."

Indeed, this belief that corporations and the superrich have a special understanding of public policy not enjoyed by ordinary mortals still shows up in the arguments of campaign finance law opponents. Bradley Smith, a former Federal Election Commission chair and a leading conservative advocate of loosening laws governing money in politics, argues that it's not a problem that the very wealthy account for such a huge proportion of political money today, because such people are "more likely to have made their money in the private sector . . . more likely to have management experience, more likely to understand the impact of regulation on business, and more likely to have thought seriously about policy than the public at large." These donors, says Smith, are also "more likely to have made their wealth in the traditional manufacturing and natural resource industries, i.e. those industries that ultimately create the 'good-paying manufacturing jobs' that everybody seems to want for blue collar workers."

IF TEAPOT DOME had shown that the first round of reforms was no panacea, Watergate made clear that a more forceful approach was urgently needed. President Richard Nixon's 1972 reelection campaign pushed the envelope in using dubiously legal accounting structures to solicit business contributions—relying in part on the fact that existing campaign finance laws essentially had no enforcement mechanism. In 1974, in the wake of the scandal, Congress strictly limited the amounts that individuals, parties, or political action committees could contribute to candidates, beefed up disclosure requirements, created a public financing system for presidential campaigns, and established the Federal Election Commission to enforce campaign finance laws. This was perhaps the high-water mark for efforts to reduce the influence of money in politics. For the first time, campaign finance regulations had teeth.

The new era meant that those who wanted to ensure a major role in elections for corporations and the megarich would have to challenge these restrictions forthrightly, rather than just quietly skirting them as they'd often done before. But getting Congress to repeal the rules was a political nonstarter. They were overwhelmingly popular, passing with bipartisan majorities in both houses. And that fall voters, still angry over Watergate, sent a massive new wave of reform-minded lawmakers, overwhelmingly Democrats, to Washington.

That left the courts. Just a year after the new rules passed, a challenge to them based in part on the claim that political spending deserves First Amendment protection made its way to the Supreme Court in *Buckley v. Valeo*. Winter himself wrote the First Amendment section of the challengers' brief. A lower court had upheld the rules, offering as it did so a ringing endorsement of the importance of ensuring political equality. "It would be strange indeed," the court found, "if, by extrapolation outward from the basic rights of individuals, the wealthy few could claim a constitutional guarantee to a stronger political voice than the unwealthy many because they are able to give and spend more money."

But the Supreme Court, now far more conservative than it had been during the 1950s and '60s, saw things differently. During oral arguments, Justice Potter Stewart, a staunch conservative, restated Winter's core point concisely: "Money is speech and speech is money, whether it is buying television or radio time or newspaper advertising." In a complicated, multipart 1976 ruling, the justices largely signed on to this view.

The free speech argument pioneered by Winter was central to *Buckley*. But the Court went further. It drew a distinction between contributions and expenditures, ruling that limits on the former but not the latter were constitutional, because spending limits couldn't be said to help stop corruption, which it found to be the *only* permissible justification for limits on political money. Trying to create rough political equality among Americans—the obvious and broadly supported animating rationale for campaign finance reforms since the nineteenth century—was no longer constitutional. As the esteemed constitutional law scholar Laurence Tribe put it, the ruling reflected a "distinctly nonegalitarian vision of the role of government and the role of elections."

Under the logic of *Buckley,* the Court began to further chip away at campaign finance laws, first allowing corporations to make contributions to ballot initiative campaigns, then signing off on what came to be known as "soft money"—contributions that went to political parties rather than candidates and therefore weren't subject to the same limits. By the end of the century, the public financing system for presidential campaigns created as part of the 1974 reforms had essentially fallen apart.

In response, for perhaps the first time ever, ordinary Americans mobilized to change the way political campaigns are financed. Arizona's public financing law, passed by voters, helped set the stage. John McCain centered his 2000 bid for president around the issue. A New Hampshire grandmother walked across the country to build support for change at the national level. Finally, in 2002, Congress passed the McCain-Feingold law, which banned soft money and took several other steps to lessen the influence of big money on campaigns. Once again, it seemed, momentum was on the side of those looking to lessen the influence of corporations and the wealthy.

But the victory would prove short-lived.

IN SEPTEMBER 1988 an independent campaign committee produced and aired perhaps the most devastating political attack ad ever created. It told the story of Willie Horton, a convicted murderer who had received a weekend furlough from prison under a Massachusetts program supported by then-governor Michael Dukakis, only to commit rape and armed robbery. The ad, which prominently featured a mug shot of the African-American Horton, played perfectly on white voters' racialized fears about violent crime. Six weeks after it aired, Dukakis was crushed by George H. W. Bush in the presidential election, winning just ten states plus the District of Columbia.

The prime mover behind the ad was a conservative operative named Floyd Brown. Four years later Brown teamed up with a man named David Bossie on what they hoped would be another political hit job, this time aimed at keeping Bush in office. They tried to substantiate a rumor that Bill Clinton had had an affair with a young woman, Susann Coleman, who had committed suicide while pregnant back in 1977. At one point Bossie trailed Coleman's mother to a U.S. Army hospital where she was visiting her sick husband to badger her with questions about her daughter's suicide. Another time Brown called Coleman's sister—who secretly recorded the call and gave the audio to a CBS News reporter—to ask whether Coleman had been depressed or suicidal.

"Just leave my family alone," the sister pleaded.

"You're making it so difficult for me to leave your family out of it," Brown replied. Even Bush's notoriously hardball campaign distanced itself from Brown and Bossie, calling them "the lowest forms of life."

By this time the two men were the leaders of a group called Citizens United, which Brown had founded to coordinate new political attacks against Democrats. By 2008 Bossie ran Citizens United on his own. That year the group's big play to influence the presidential election was a crude documentary called *Hillary: The Movie*, which dredged up various sketchily sourced 1990s-era allegations about Hillary Clinton, who at that time looked likely to be the Democratic nominee. It featured, among many other accusers, Kathleen Willey, who a decade earlier had told *60 Minutes* that Bill Clinton sexually harassed her in the White House and who now claimed in the movie that Hillary once plotted to assassinate her cat.

Citizens United wanted to run the movie as a cable video on-demand and to advertise it on TV, but the Federal Election Commission held that both activities violated the McCain-Feingold law, which banned corporations from running TV ads that mentioned a candidate within thirty days of a primary election. After Bossie and Citizens United sued, and a federal appeals panel sided with the FEC, the issue came before the Supreme Court in early 2009.

The lawyer Bossie had hired to handle the case up to this

point, Jim Bopp, was an Indiana-based movement conservative, an RNC official, and a crusading opponent of campaign
finance laws. It was thanks to Bopp's bold vision that McCain-
Feingold was already riddled with a major hole. In 2007, in *FEC
v. Wisconsin Right to Life*, Bopp had convinced the Court's five
conservatives to strike down the law's ban on corporate-funded
issue ads, even those clearly meant to influence an election. The
ruling surprised many observers. After all, just four years earlier
the justices had largely rejected another challenge to McCain-
Feingold—this one brought by the Republican Senate leader,
Mitch McConnell, a longtime foe of campaign finance regulation. But the Court had shifted rightward since the McConnell
case. In 2006 Samuel Alito, a committed conservative, replaced
Justice Sandra Day O'Connor, who had sided with the liberals against McConnell. Alito became the fifth vote to weaken
McCain-Feingold.

Still, Bossie felt his organization's future was on the line,
and he was more interested in getting a ruling that allowed him
to distribute his movie than in obliterating campaign finance
law going forward. A lower court had been unimpressed by
Bopp's expansive First Amendment claim on behalf of Citizens
United—the judge had openly laughed at his attempt to compare
the tacky film to a *60 Minutes* news story in order to claim that
it deserved the same First Amendment protections. So Bossie
ditched Bopp and brought in Ted Olson, the conservative super-
lawyer with a reputation as a skilled litigator, not an ideologue.

True to form, Olson made a narrow, cautious argument. He
told the justices he wasn't asking for them to declare any part of
the McCain-Feingold law unconstitutional—after all, the Court
had largely upheld it six years earlier, in the case brought by

McConnell. Rather, Olson was offering the reasonable claim that the law didn't apply to a movie that was accessible through an on-demand system, since any viewers would have made an affirmative choice to watch it rather than being bombarded against their will with a campaign commercial while watching TV. Roberts duly wrote an opinion for the majority that accepted this limited argument and not much more. Had that opinion seen the light of day, Citizens United would have been able to run its anti-Hillary movie, but the case would have had little broader impact.

But limiting the scope of the case was the last thing the Court's conservatives appeared to want. Justice Anthony Kennedy wrote a separate concurrence that went much further, saying that not only were McCain-Feingold's restrictions on political ads close to an election unconstitutional, so too were any limits on political spending by corporations. The three other conservative justices made clear that they agreed with Kennedy. So Roberts withdrew his own opinion and turned Kennedy's far-reaching concurrence into the Court's official decision.

But the chief justice tends to worry about the Court's reputation. And he knew that Kennedy's opinion addressed issues so far beyond the scope of the case as it had been argued that issuing it would have opened the justices up to charges of judicial activism—that they were seizing the chance to make a sweeping ruling on questions that hadn't been raised, and in doing so, striking down legislation passed not long ago by democratic majorities. So Roberts now withdrew this opinion, too. Then, as Jeffrey Toobin detailed in a 2012 *New Yorker* story, Roberts expanded the scope of the case.

To do so, he ordered that *Citizens United* be reargued that fall and ensured that this time the "Questions Presented"—a set of instructions in which the Court lays out the issues it wants lawyers on both sides to address—would be much broader. Roberts was confident that none of the conservative justices would change their minds about the outcome, and now it would be harder for the Court's critics to claim that the opinion had overreached. In effect, the Court had fixed things so it could take up Jim Bopp's sweeping arguments rather than Ted Olson's narrow ones.

Roberts again had Kennedy write the opinion for the majority. Released in January 2010, that opinion faithfully reflected the conservative orthodoxy on money in politics—that there's essentially no distinction between money that pays for political speech, and speech itself. To limit the former is to limit the latter and thus violates the First Amendment. Indeed, in laws that regulated political spending by corporations, Kennedy seemed to see a massive government scheme to silence important sectors of society. "The Government has muffled the voices that best represent the most significant segments of the economy," he wrote. "By suppressing the speech of manifold corporations, both for-profit and non-profit, the Government prevents their voices and viewpoints from reaching the public and advising voters on which persons or entities are hostile to their interests." (The use of *hostile,* of course, suggests Kennedy assumed—pretty much accurately—that corporations would want to pay only for negative ads, not positive ones.)

Roberts's maneuvering wasn't entirely successful in warding off criticism about judicial activism. "Five Justices were unhappy with the limited nature of the case before us, so they changed the case to give themselves an opportunity to change the law," wrote Justice John Paul Stevens in a stinging dissent, adding, "At bottom, the Court's opinion is thus a rejection of the common sense of the American people, who have recognized a need to prevent corporations from undermining self-government since the founding, and who have fought against the distinctive corrupting potential of corporate electioneering since the days of Theodore Roosevelt."

But the implication of Kennedy's opinion was clear. Most of McCain-Feingold was struck down, and corporations now had a right to spend an unlimited amount of money on politics. And it wasn't just corporations. Based on the broad antiregulation philosophy that Kennedy had laid out, a federal court ruled two months later in *SpeechNow.org v. FEC* that individual wealthy Americans could make unlimited contributions to super PACs in support of candidates—a ruling whose immediate impact was perhaps even more earth-shattering than that of *Citizens United*. The conservative justices weren't finished, either. The following year they would weaken the Arizona public financing law. Then, in *McCutcheon v. FEC* in 2014, the Court scrapped limits on the total amount one person can give to multiple candidates or committees, again finding that those limits can't be said to deter corruption.

Perhaps more important, the Roberts Court narrowed the definition of the kind of corruption that lawmakers can legitimately try to stop. Since *Buckley*, that definition had seemed to be widening. Foes of campaign finance laws had long acted as though *Buckley* held that Congress could only target "quid pro quo" corruption—bribery, essentially. In fact, *Buckley* had taken care to say that quid pro quo corruption was "only the most blatant" way that moneyed interests try to influence government, suggesting that other, less direct forms of influence might also be fair game for regulation. And some subsequent decisions had seemed to expand the definition of corruption to allow campaign finance laws that in fact were aimed more at creating a level playing field. The most notable came in 1990, when the justices upheld a Michigan law barring corporations from making contributions to independent expenditure campaigns. The Court's 2003 decision mostly upholding McCain-Feingold—a law that unquestionably went far beyond stopping explicit bribery—further suggested that it was willing to take a very broad interpretation of what counts as corruption.

But in *Citizens United*, the justices seemed to have backtracked. The Arizona public financing case, in which Roberts went out of his way to emphasize the Court's absolute ban on any attempt to establish political equality, took things in the same direction. Now, in *McCutcheon*, they made it official. "Any regulation must instead target what we have called 'quid pro quo' corruption or its appearance," wrote Chief Justice Roberts, adding that he was talking about "a direct exchange of an official act for money." From here on, reformers would be fighting with one hand tied behind their backs.

IN REALITY, OF COURSE, big-money political donors don't need explicit quid pro quo deals to gain influence. And understanding why is crucial for grasping the real impact of the Court's step-by-step evisceration of limits on money in politics.

Before we get there, let's first look at the world that our new no-holds-barred campaign finance system has produced. Simply put, thanks in large part to super PACs that accept unlimited donations, the very wealthy now make up an enormous share of political contributors. In the 2014 cycle the 1 percent of the

1 percent—just under 32,000 people—accounted for $1.18 billion, or nearly 30 percent of all disclosed political donations. By June 2015, just 158 families had already contributed a total of $176 million to support 2016 presidential candidates—all but twenty backing Republicans, according to a *New York Times* analysis. The paper noted that the donors were "overwhelmingly white, rich, older, and male." Nor was this money counterbalanced by a surge of small donors: families contributing at least $100,000 accounted for well over half the money in the presidential race. "The question is whether we are in a new Gilded Age or well beyond it—to a Platinum Age," Michael Malbin of the Campaign Finance Institute told the *Times*.

In theory, of course, super PACs are barred from coordinating with campaigns, but in practice that restriction—one of the few the courts have left untouched—doesn't mean much, because campaigns have found all manner of clever ways around the ban. In 2015 a super PAC supporting John Kasich released an ad that featured the Ohio governor looking into the camera and touting his "foreign policy experience." There was no coordination, the group said, because the ad was filmed months earlier, before Kasich had announced his candidacy. Around the same time, a super PAC backing Jeb Bush hosted a series of lavish fund-raisers for him—again, before he had officially declared he was running. Ted Cruz's campaign may have gotten the most creative: it posted online raw footage of interviews with the candidate and his parents—complete with awkward outtakes—so that his super PAC could use it to produce gauzy biographical ads.

Those kinds of tricks, which clearly violate the spirit and perhaps the letter of existing campaign finance laws, might once have been stopped by an engaged FEC. But in recent years, the agency, which has three Republican and Democratic appointees each, has been all but neutered by its GOP members, who consistently have voted as a bloc against enforcing even the modest restrictions on money in politics still on the books. In November 2015 they blocked the agency from following the advice of its lawyers and banning a slew of shady super PAC tactics—including the ones employed by Bush and Kasich to skirt coordination rules. "I don't believe that they really believe in the [FEC's] real mission," the agency's chair, Ann Ravel, told me of her Republican-appointed colleagues.

Big-money donors, then, are freer to spend money on politics today than at any time for at least four decades and perhaps a century. And yet for all that, these donors haven't always gotten their way. It's become a commonplace in some quarters to say that money buys elections, or that the Roberts Court has opened elections to the highest bidder. But it's not nearly that simple. Jeb Bush's super PAC may have raised over $100 million in just the first half of 2015, but it didn't do him much good in the race for the GOP presidential nomination. In 2012 a super PAC created by Karl Rove's group spent over $100 million on attack ads and finished with virtually nothing to show for it. Money can't turn a bad candidate into a good one—especially in presidential races, where the impact of big money tends to be canceled out by its presence on all sides. To be sure, money does allow *über*-wealthy individual donors to pretty much bankroll presidential campaigns on their own. Newt Gingrich's 2012 presidential bid was essentially a production of billionaire casino magnate Sheldon Adelson, who gave around $20 million to a pro-Gingrich super PAC, allowing Newt to hang around in the race for far longer than he'd otherwise have been able to. But, of course, Gingrich didn't win.

Instead, money exerts its influence on our politics in a subtler but no less harmful way. Outright bribery of the kind that Bobby Raymond and his colleagues committed usually isn't necessary, because elected officials already understand that consistently acting against the interests of their biggest donors will jeopardize their future ability to raise money and run viable campaigns. And so, perhaps without even realizing it, they're far more responsive to the needs of big contributors and the broader socioeconomic class that those donors tend to come from.

It's not hard to see how this plays out. There's a clear consensus among tax policy experts, for instance, that the carried interest loophole, which lets hedge funds and private equity firms save billions in taxes, should be closed. It survives not because Wall Street villains have bribed politicians but because, in the 2012 and 2014 cycles, financial interests spent over $1 billion to help elect politicians from both parties, and lawmakers are wary of offending an industry that plays a major role in funding their campaigns. And have you ever wondered why virtually every GOP presidential candidate offered a tax plan that, according to independent studies, hugely benefits the rich? Ted Cruz, Marco Rubio, and even the nominally populist Donald Trump all gave the top 1 percent of earners an after-tax increase of at least 10 percent, far more than any of them gave the middle class (a whopping 40 percent of the benefits of Rubio's plan went to the 1 percent, one widely respected policy group found). It's not because voters favor it. A 2014 Gallup poll found that just 13 percent of respondents said the rich pay too much in taxes, compared to 61 percent who said they pay too little. That latter number hasn't dropped below 55 percent in over two decades. Even among Republicans, the number who said the rich pay too little was more than double the number who said they pay too much.

But the very wealthy who benefit from these policies also happen to make up a huge chunk of Republican political donors—meaning it's not hard to understand why politicians dependent on those donors embrace these ideas. Or consider Adelson. His largesse on Gingrich's behalf in 2012 meant that the next time around Republican candidates lined up to win his favor. To pretend that this hasn't given him more influence than your average American over their policy positions is to close one's eyes to reality. In 2014 New Jersey governor Chris Christie personally apologized to Adelson, a major backer of Israel's right-wing government, after referring to the "occupied territories"—a term that's been used by the U.S. government but that conservative supporters of Israel don't like.

This dynamic might be less destructive if the policy views of the ultrarich were generally in line with those of most Americans. But there's convincing evidence that people who make a lot of money—surprise, surprise—care much less about helping the poor than those who don't. An authoritative 2013 study found that 78 percent of Americans think the minimum wage should be high enough to keep people out of poverty, but just 40 percent of the very wealthy—those making over $1 million a year—agree. And it found that 68 percent of the public think the government should ensure that everyone who wants to work can find a job—an idea often treated as beyond the pale in mainstream political debate—compared to just 19 percent of the very wealthy who think so.

In other words, the barrage of political money from corporations and the superwealthy isn't generally buying elections outright—but it's helping to shift policy outcomes in a more conservative direction, especially on the economic issues that are at the center of our political divide. As such, it works in concert with the restrictions on voting that have been pushed by the same broad movement and green-lighted by the same conservative Supreme Court majority. To many observers who are committed to an egalitarian notion of democracy, both have had the effect of further quieting the voices of certain groups of Americans—racial minorities, the poor, the young, and women—who already are often alienated from the political process and who are much less likely to be, or to have ties to, large-scale political donors.

"What is happening, clearly, is the people who have access and are able to express their views, those are people who are able to change the discussion," Ravel, the FEC chair, said. "And so there's going to be this whole group of people who are kind of like a permanent class of outsiders." These disfavored groups "are never going to have an opportunity to run for office, because they can't access the money," Ravel said. "They aren't going to participate in the political system, and they are dropping out and not voting. This is another mechanism for trying to eliminate them from the conversation."

The good news is that—just as happened during the Gilded Age and after the failure of the Watergate reforms—ordinary people are noticing. The success of Bernie Sanders and Trump in the 2016 presidential race, each of whom has assailed the campaign finance system for giving outsize sway to wealthy donors, is perhaps the best evidence that Americans want change. Polling shows the same thing. Eighty-four percent of respondents to a 2015 survey said there's too much corporate money in politics, and two-thirds said the wealthy have more chance to influence the process than do other people. And 78 percent of respondents to a different poll that year said the *Citizens United* ruling should be overturned, compared to 17 percent who said it was a good decision. "I'm stunned," one constitutional law professor told Bloomberg News in response to those numbers. "What it suggests is that *Citizens United* has become a symbol for what people perceive to be a much larger problem, which is the undue influence of wealth in politics."

But Bill Maurer, the lawyer who successfully challenged the Arizona public financing law before the Supreme Court, drew a different lesson from those results: "It's a good thing we have a Constitution that protects the rights of individuals from the whims of majorities—including large majorities," Maurer wrote. "In fact, it is probably when majorities are at their most uni-fied that the protections of the Constitution are at their most important."

Chapter 3

WHAT HAPPENED IN DENTON

B y early 2014, a lot of people in Denton had had enough.

Over the last decade, oil and gas companies had drilled more than two hundred fracking wells in the city of around 115,000, which lies forty miles north of Dallas. For a while most of the residents seemed fine with it. After all, this was Texas, where ever-expanding energy development is a way of life. And fracking, a technique for extracting natural gas from shale rock, didn't seem all that different from the traditional oil and gas drilling that had powered the state's economy for over a century. There were even wells across the street from Apogee Stadium, home of the Mean Green of the University of North Texas.

Gradually, though, attitudes shifted. More was becoming known about the potential health and environmental effects of fracking, which has been linked to dangerous levels of air and water pollution. Then around 2010, developers drilled three new wells in quick succession across the street from a playground, a hospital, and a row of homes, respectively. In response, the city council issued new regulations aimed at keeping fracking away from residential areas. But the industry essentially ignored them, claiming that any wells built before the rules went into effect were exempt. That's when a group of Denton residents—among them a nurse, a professor at the local university, and a Meals on Wheels volunteer—came together to launch a campaign to ban fracking in their city.

The activists would be vastly outspent by oil and gas interests, who implied as part of a high-profile PR campaign, and without evidence, that supporters of a ban were in Vladimir Putin's pocket and were trying to protect Russia's share of the global natural gas market. And the activists didn't have a lot of experience with the political process, to put it mildly. "We had no idea what we were doing," acknowledged Adam Briggle, the university professor who helped lead the effort.

But they were committed—driven by the twin beliefs that fracking could pose a serious threat to their own and their families' health, and that Denton's future should be determined by its citizens, not by outside corporations. They got two hundred people to pack a local bar owned by a supporter for a campaign kickoff event. They gathered signatures to get a fracking ban on the ballot, then set about convincing their neighbors to vote for it in November. They met every Tuesday at a local restaurant to plot strategy. Musicians, artists, and puppeteers gave performances to help raise awareness. Briggle drew on his expertise as an environmental studies PhD to educate Dentonites about fracking's potential danger. Everyone pitched in.

In the end, it wasn't close: 59 percent of voters approved the measure, and Denton became the first Texas city to ban fracking. The intensity of the ban's supporters was off the charts: one man said he'd been hospitalized after suffering a heart attack, but broke out to vote for the ban. "The democratic process is alive and well in Denton," the city's mayor declared. Briggle and his fellow activists celebrated into the night at the bar where they had launched the campaign.

It was an inspiring victory for grassroots organizing and local democracy. But it didn't last long.

At 9:08 the following morning, with Briggle still nursing a hangover, lawyers for the oil and gas industry, which feared that Denton's move could prompt other local governments to pass similar laws, sued to prevent the ban from going into effect. The state agency in charge of natural resources filed its own suit later that day, calling the ban unconstitutional and claiming that it unfairly deprived Texas of profits from mineral rights on state-owned land. Then, in case that didn't work, the industry tried another tactic: it pulled out all the stops to get state lawmakers to reverse the ban—the will of Denton's voters be damned.

Saying that the oil and gas industry has some sway in the Texas legislature is sort of like saying LeBron James is a pretty good basketball player. By early 2015, Republican lawmakers were competing with one another to introduce bills that would undo the Denton measure. Some foes of the ban argued that Denton voters lacked the sophistication to weigh in on technical matters like fracking, which were best left to government and industry experts. In a newspaper column, Christi Craddick, the chair of the Texas Railroad Commission, which regulates the oil and gas industry in the state, criticized the "misinformation and sensationalism" that had clouded the vote and touted her agency as an "informed partner" that could help broker a solution allowing Denton to continue to enjoy the economic benefits of "our state's most iconic and lucrative industry." At a public event, Craddick was blunter: "Local control's great in a lot of respects. But I'm the expert on oil and gas. The city of Denton is not." Others warned that the industry needed one uniform set of rules in Texas. "We don't need a patchwork approach to drilling regulations across the state," George P. Bush—Jeb's son—a former energy investment consultant who was campaigning to be the state's top regulator of mineral rights, had said over the summer as support for the ban grew among Dentonites.

In the end, lawmakers coalesced around a bill, known as HB40, that preempted the authority of local governments to regulate a wide range of energy development activities, including fracking. It was approved 122–18 in the House and by a wide margin in the Senate, too. A white paper sent by the city of Denton pleading its case was ignored. Governor Greg Abbott quickly signed HB40 into law, echoing George P. Bush in saying that it was needed to avoid "a patchwork quilt of regulations that . . . differ from county to county or city to city." The bill, Abbott added, does a "profound job of protecting private property rights."

Faced with the prospect of a costly lawsuit it was now all but certain to lose, Denton reluctantly repealed its ban in June 2015. By then fracking had already begun at a new site northwest of the city's downtown. To Denton's activists, the message was all too clear: when powerful interests are on the other side, the views of ordinary people don't count for much.

"I feel like they kind of just slammed the door and locked it, and I don't know how to break through that," Briggle told me. "I was worried about fracking to start with. But now I'm worried about democracy."

WHAT HAPPENED IN Denton wasn't just about oil and gas interests and their outsize influence in Texas's government. It was
also a particularly ruthless example of a new kind of conservative power grab.

In December 2015 Jacki Pick, an executive at a Koch-funded
think tank and a host on Glenn Beck's radio network, gave a
presentation at a Scottsdale, Arizona, meeting of the American
Legislative Exchange Council (ALEC), the powerful and secre-
tive corporate lobby group. Pick warned of a growing trend:
local-level regulations that posed a threat to corporate profits.
She used the Denton fracking ban as a case study. To Pick, it
was evidence of the danger of too much local democracy. She
characterized the grassroots activism behind the ban as just
"unemployed college kids with lots of time on their hands" (in
fact, the ban appears to have been supported by a pretty representative cross-section of Denton residents) and said activism
like this "needs to be shut down" in other places as it had been
in Denton. The students, Pick added, "don't live there, don't
pay taxes there, yet they're deciding these issues," and she urged
her audience of business executives and their legislative supporters to "get out in front of these activists who are ginning up
discontent."

In recent years, Republican-led states from Arizona to
Florida have declared war on local democracy. With help from
deep-pocketed business interests often working through ALEC,
they've launched a coordinated campaign in favor of state laws
that preempt those passed by cities and counties. It's an assault
that deliberately undermines the power of local governments

to determine the direction of their own communities and rides roughshod over the principles of local control that conservatives have traditionally espoused. And it's happening at a time when cities are emerging as all-too-rare bastions of enlightened, people-centric governing. As such, it exemplifies, perhaps better than any other development, how the right's game plan for fighting off progressive policy goals increasingly relies on trying to hold back the democratic tide. "I think it is the time of greatest risk to local democracy that has probably ever existed," Mark Pertschuk of Grassroots Change, which supports local democracy efforts around the country, told me in reference to the push for preemption. "I see it as a fundamental threat."

Texas has actually been something of a late arrival to the preemption game, which has been played across the country in some form for three decades. Like many of corporate America's most effective and controversial lobbying tactics, preemption was pioneered by the tobacco industry. Back in the mid-1980s, Big Tobacco grew worried about the spread of local antismoking ordinances, which were being pushed by a powerful citizens' movement. The industry feared that the kind of "patchwork quilt" of local laws that Abbott would later invoke would hugely complicate its lobbying efforts, making it fight hundreds of small-scale skirmishes and potentially building momentum for broader regulations.

Soon the tobacco industry hit on a solution. In 1986 it successfully lobbied the Florida legislature to pass a law that took away the authority of local governments to institute antismoking ordinances. (Public health advocates ruefully referred to it as the Tobacco Industry Relief Act.) From there, the strategy went nationwide. Within a few years, the industry would push legislation to ban local smoke-free ordinances in virtually every state in the country. Twenty states ultimately passed such laws. "While we're not married to any particular form of pre-emption language, we're dead serious about achieving pre-emption in all 50 states," a Philip Morris executive wrote in an internal memo in 1994.

In the long run, preemption didn't really work out for Big Tobacco. Over the last decade, many of those twenty states have repealed their smoke-free preemption laws. Those moves came after public health groups waged vigorous state-level campaigns pointing to the growing evidence of the dangers of secondhand smoke, and after many bars and restaurants, seeing that the smoking bans didn't hurt business, dropped their opposition to them.

But the broader preemption strategy would prove more enduring. In the 1990s the National Rifle Association took it up. After big cities began passing increasingly strict gun laws, the gun lobby managed to get forty-six states to enact gun control preemption laws. Other industries joined them. Alcohol interests, for instance, persuaded California to prevent counties from banning the sale of booze at gas stations. And nineteen states, pushed by the telecom industry, enacted laws banning cities from providing free municipal broadband. But it wasn't until a few years into the Obama era that things kicked into a much higher gear. By this time, individual industries weren't waging these fights alone.

In 1973 a staffer in the Illinois statehouse, with help from the legendary conservative activist Paul Weyrich, founded a group called the Conservative Caucus of State Legislators, which acted as a kind of dating agency for large corporations and the conservative state lawmakers who loved them. It was part of a broader push by the right to build institutions that could counter the rise of big government—that year Weyrich would also help create the Heritage Foundation with a similar goal.* The caucus's leaders soon decided that the term *conservative* was unpopular, so the name was changed to the American Legislative Exchange Council, or ALEC.

At first, ALEC pushed a grab bag of right-wing causes. But gradually it narrowed its focus to issues that would directly impact the bottom line of its corporate members, acting as an umbrella group for their lobbying campaigns. Today ALEC drafts cookie-cutter business-friendly legislation, then shares it with the state legislators—nearly all of them Republicans—who make up its membership, urging them to introduce their own versions. One ALEC-affiliated lawmaker is said to have approvingly compared the whole arrangement to a football team, with the legislators as the players and the corporate lobbyists as the coaches. The group's funders include Exxon, the American Petroleum Institute, and foundations run by Charles Koch and other right-wing billionaires like beer heir Pete Coors.

The Tea Party wave of 2010 that gave Republicans full control of a slew of state governments had another effect, too. Stymied in Washington and now in many of the states, progressives increasingly turned their focus to the local level, where they sought measures that would, among other things, improve conditions for workers, curb pollution, and bar discrimination. As

---

* Weyrich's views on voting should come as no surprise. "I don't want everybody to vote," he told a conservative conference in 1980. "Our leverage in the elections quite candidly goes up as the voting populace goes down."

these campaigns succeeded, they inspired copycat efforts across the country. That meant the threat posed by local government to corporate interests was genuinely increasing. In response, ALEC and its industry partners came to a realization similar to the one that dawned on Big Tobacco in the 1980s: local government was where the game would be won or lost, and preemption was the most valuable tool in their toolkit.

Suddenly it was open season on any local law that powerful industries didn't like. Wisconsin, newly under all-Republican control, soon became a preemption hotspot. It banned local public health measures that addressed restaurant portion size. It banned local regulation of ride-sharing services like Uber, instead creating statewide standards many Democrats criticized as too lax. Mississippi—the state with the nation's highest obesity rate—passed an even broader measure on portion size and nutrition, barring local governments from requiring restaurants or other food sellers to disclose nutritional information to consumers. Oklahoma passed a fracking ban ban (you read that right) like Texas's, and Colorado officials have sued two cities that outlawed fracking, arguing that state law already bars them from doing so. Arizona and Florida banned local laws that prevent fast-food companies from putting toys in their meals as a way to lure kids. After Salt Lake City made restaurants serve bicyclists in their drive-through lanes, Utah banned that, too.

But nowhere was the move for preemption explicitly laid out from the top the way it was in Texas. Even before he took office as governor in 2015, Abbott signaled that he was readying to launch a broad assault on local democracy. "Texas is being California-ized, and you may not even be noticing it," he said in a major policy speech just before being sworn in. "Unchecked over-regulation by cities will turn the Texas miracle into the California nightmare."* After Abbott's call to arms, Texas Republicans sponsored more than twenty-five different preemption bills in the 2015 legislative session. There were bans on banning plastic bags, and a ban on local smoking ordinances of the kind pushed by the tobacco industry for three decades. There was even a ban on cities requiring landlords to accept payment via federal housing vouchers—a direct response to an Austin law that aimed to desegregate housing in the city. That one ended up passing, eliminating a key tool in Austin's effort to combat a decades-long legacy of redlining and housing discrimination.

Many of the bills were broader. One, introduced by Phil King, a Republican legislator who serves as ALEC's national chair, would have given the state's attorney general the power to reject any ballot initiative proposed by a city before voters were allowed to weigh in. But even that measure paled in comparison to one introduced by Don Huffines, a freshman senator and real estate and car dealership billionaire from the Dallas area. Known as the "nuclear option," Huffines's bill banned any local regulation that conflicts with, or is more stringent than, state law—which could have effectively ended any real policy-making role for local government in Texas. In the end, after a frantic opposition campaign from mayors and city councils, none of the broader measures passed—leaving some conservative lawmakers vowing to come back for more. "We didn't do enough," Representative Matt Rinaldi said at the end of the session. "We left

---

* For many conservatives, California is the poster child for the dangers of excessive regulation. As he ran for governor, Abbott would often get a laugh by darkly invoking "people streaming over the border every single day," before deadpanning, "They are Californians." Many were small-business owners, he would add, attracted to Texas's hands-off regulatory climate.

open the issues where cities were curtailing the personal liberties of their citizens and going outside the bounds of what they are expected to do."

This drive to weaken local government was particularly ironic, of course, coming from Texas conservatives, who have led the way in turning states' rights into a weapon to use against the president's agenda, from immigration to Obamacare. At one point when he was the state's governor, Rick Perry even mused about secession. And hasn't the right been telling us for years that, as the Founders understood, government works best when it's closest to the people? If states are better than Washington at tailoring policy to fit people's needs, why wouldn't local governments be better at it than states?

To understand the real answer, it helps to first imagine a situation in which the policy implications of local control are reversed. It's easy for progressives to oppose preemption when local government is helping working people or strengthening environmental protections and the state is pushing in the opposite direction. But we didn't wring our hands about the threat to local democracy when conservative counties were forced to go along with state laws or court rulings legalizing same-sex marriage.

The reality is, few of us believe local governments should get to decide everything for themselves. Most progressives think certain rights—the right to be protected from discrimination based on race, gender, or sexual orientation, for instance—supersede the democratic process. But that's exactly what many conservative supporters of preemption argue, too—they just have very different rights in mind. Echoing John Adams and his allies, they see private property rights, and more broadly, the right of free enterprise, as similarly nonnegotiable. (As we'll see in chapter 5, there's even a growing legal movement to have courts give these rights stronger constitutional protection.)

As he signed HB40 into law, Abbott said the ban on fracking bans was needed to avoid "an encroachment on private property rights at the local level." Huffines, the author of Texas's "nuclear option" bill, was more colorful. "I don't consider local control a blank check to just trample the liberties of the business community or their citizens," he said at a hearing. "To me, tyranny from your neighbor or a local government or a dictator of a foreign country is still tyranny." Or as State Representative Rinaldi put it: "Liberty always trumps local control."

Of course, seeing preemption as a matter of principled ideology in some ways gives its architects too much credit. Just as partisanship explains most, though not all, of the war on voting, the drive for preemption is mainly being led by well-connected corporate interests aiming to use their massive political influence to protect their bottom lines. Perhaps the best illustration is the fight over workers' wages and benefits—with ALEC and the restaurant industry at the center of it.

A DECADE OR SO ago advocates for the working poor became concerned that low-wage employees—that is, workers who make the minimum wage or close to it—risked being docked pay or fired if they called in sick. The threat of flu-stricken fast-food workers sneezing or vomiting on burgers after being denied time off turned the issue into a public health problem, too. So in several cities across the country, grassroots campaigns took off to require employers to provide paid sick leave.

Ellen Bravo was teaching a class at the University of

Wisconsin–Milwaukee at the time, and many of her students worked in fast-food jobs to get by. "I would ask them: 'Raise your hand if you've ever called in sick and been told 'get in here anyway,' " Bravo, an advocate for family-friendly leave policies, told me. "Invariably, every semester, almost every student would raise their hand." Like many struggling cities, Milwaukee has a large share of low-wage workers. Many of them are in the fast-food industry, and a particularly strong coalition for paid sick days emerged there. It included groups representing working women, seniors, people with disabilities, asthma sufferers, and immigrants, all of whom recognized that their constituencies had a stake in the issue. Like Adam Briggle and his friends in Denton, the Milwaukee activists gathered signatures to get a voter initiative requiring paid sick days on the city ballot in November 2008. It passed with almost 70 percent approval, buoyed by support from minorities and young people who had turned out in huge numbers to vote for Barack Obama.

The local chamber of commerce, backed by the Wisconsin Restaurant Association, sued—claiming, among other things, that Milwaukee's law amounted to an illegal attempt to raise the minimum wage. After years of litigation, an appeals court ruled for the city. Finally, in early 2011, the paid-sick-days measure was set to go into effect.

But as in Denton, the industry had hedged its bets in case the ruling didn't go its way. That January Scott Walker and a Republican legislature had taken control of the state. Two weeks after the appeals court ruled, lawmakers approved a restaurant-industry-backed measure that barred cities from passing laws on family leave issues—thereby neatly preempting Milwaukee's paid-sick-leave requirement. Paid-sick-leave supporters showed up to testify at a hearing, but the Republican majority didn't seem interested in listening to what ordinary people had to say. "They were walking in and out of the room and looking at their phones," said Bravo. "They weren't paying attention at all." Walker signed the bill into law, blasting "patchwork government mandates" that stifle job creation.

"People said, 'Wait a minute, didn't we just vote for this thing? And we won. How can they just undo it like that? How can they steal it from us?'" said Bravo, who had helped lead the sick leave campaign. But as dispiriting as Wisconsin's experience was, things were about to get worse for supporters of paid sick leave and local democracy. ALEC was about to enter the picture.

Six months after Walker and the legislature killed Milwaukee's paid sick leave, nearly two thousand industry lobbyists and conservative state lawmakers from around the country gathered at the swanky New Orleans Marriott, not far from Bourbon Street, for ALEC's annual meeting. Bobby Jindal, Dick Armey, and Art Laffer—known as the father of supply-side economics, and a member of ALEC's "Board of Scholars"—addressed the overwhelmingly white crowd. A convention booklet included a long list of corporate partners, among them Walmart, Chevron, ExxonMobil, the drug industry lobby group PhRMA, and Koch Industries. At a meeting of ALEC's "Labor and Business Regulation Subcommittee"—co-chaired by a lobbyist for YUM! Brands, which owns KFC, Pizza Hut, and Taco Bell—lawmakers were given copies of the Wisconsin paid-sick-leave preemption bill signed by Walker, a former ALEC member. They also received a map prepared by the National Restaurant Association, showing the growing number of cities and counties that had proposed or passed paid-sick-day laws. The message was clear:

industry wanted versions of the Wisconsin bill in as many states as possible.

Since that New Orleans meeting, twelve other states—all Republican-controlled—have passed sick-leave preemption laws similar to Wisconsin's, with restaurant industry lobbyists or ALEC-affiliated legislators, or both, playing key roles. Alabama's version, passed in 2014, was the top priority of the Alabama Restaurant and Hospitality Alliance. Getting the bill through was "not an easy task, since granting more leave time has been a topic promoted in the media," the trade association bragged to its members. "Those in the food-service and hotel industry in states that do not have this protection have experienced hardship from the passage of such local laws." The hardship experienced by the restaurant workers unable to take a day off when they're sick naturally went unmentioned.

OF COURSE, FOR many food service workers, the most urgent problem they face isn't a lack of paid sick leave—it's poverty wages. And some states have banned cities from taking action there, too.

Remember that mock budget that McDonald's created for its employees, which showed that they could easily get by on fast-food wages—as long as they worked a second job and spent just twenty dollars a month on health care and nothing on child care, clothing, groceries, or gas? The ensuing press coverage, along with similar, more personal stories, have shined a light on fast-food workers' struggles to get by while their corporate employers generate billions in profits. And so since 2012, responding to powerful grassroots and labor-backed campaigns, thirty-three cities or counties representing well over ten million people combined have raised their minimum wage laws higher than the state or federal level. A few, including Los Angeles, San Francisco, Oakland, and Seattle, have gone all the way up to fifteen dollars an hour—more than double the federal minimum.

ALEC has taken notice. "Perhaps the biggest threat comes from the local level," Cara Sullivan, an official with the group, acknowledged at a meeting of an ALEC-affiliated organization last year, referring to minimum wage hikes. State-level preemption, she added, was one of ALEC's favored responses.

At least twenty-one states have passed such laws—most in the last few years and after intense lobbying by ALEC or the restaurant industry. Oklahoma's 2014 law came after a vigorous campaign by Oklahoma City activists to raise the city's minimum wage to $10.10 an hour, from $7.25. Before the measure could make it to the ballot, legislators passed a law that banned local governments from raising the minimum wage *or* requiring employers to provide paid sick leave or vacations. It was signed into law by Governor Mary Fallin, like Walker a former ALEC member; she had given the keynote speech at the group's meeting the previous year.

Michigan's law, passed last year and dubbed the "Death Star" by opponents, achieved the same sick leave/minimum wage twofer while also banning a host of other local employment protections, including bans on antigay discrimination that had already been passed by thirty-eight of the state's municipalities. After a public outcry, the bill was modified so as not to apply retroactively. Still, one progressive leader described it as part of a "co-ordinated attack on democracy" launched by Governor Rick Snyder and the Republican legislature.

Of course, states and cities have always clashed over the limits of their authority. But states looking to preempt local minimum wage laws are defying the popular will with a particular boldness. Polls show most people support raising the minimum wage significantly higher than the federal $7.25 mark–and not only in liberal West Coast cities. Increasingly, Americans understand that wage growth has slowed dramatically, as an ever-larger share of profits goes to those at the top. And the message that everyone who works should be able to support themselves is clear, simple, and easily understood. That's why the more input voters are allowed, the better the prospects for a higher minimum wage. When, in November 2014, a wage boost was put directly before voters in four deep-red states–Arkansas, Nebraska, Alaska, and South Dakota–it passed across the board, even as conservative Republicans were elected to office. By contrast, the most effective strategy the other side has come up with to keep the minimum wage low relies very directly on limiting democracy's reach.

"You measure democracy not only by the fairness of elections, but also by what's the scope of life over which people can exercise democratic control," Gordon Lafer, an economist at the University of Oregon who has studied minimum wage law and preemption, told me. "So this is kind of taking an important issue and saying: 'This one, you don't have the right to vote over.'"

IN 1995 a former tobacco industry lobbyist named Victor Crawford–a smoker since the age of thirteen–was dying of throat cancer. As part of an effort to make amends for his years peddling nicotine, he gave a remarkably candid interview to the

Journal of the American Medical Association about the industry's lobbying tactics. At one point, Crawford was asked about preemption. Why did the industry always look to take the fight away from the local level? He replied:

> We could never win at the local level. The reason is, all the health advocates, the ones that unfortunately I used to call "health Nazis," they're all local activists who run the little political organizations. They may live next door to the mayor, or the city councilman may be his or her brother-in-law, and they say, "who's this big-time lobbyist coming here to tell us what to do?" When they've got their friends and neighbors out there in the audience who want this bill, we get killed.
>
> So the Tobacco Institute and tobacco companies' first priority has always been to preempt the field. Preferably to put it all on the federal level, but if they can't do that, at least on the state level. Because the health advocates can't compete with me on a state level. They never could. On the local level, I couldn't compete with them. And that's why all your antismoking legislation without exception has started at the local level, all across the country.

Crawford's answer hit on a profound truth about democracy in America—and the dynamic he described still exists today, on everything from fracking bans to the minimum wage. Corporate lobbyists can usually use their influence to stymie or water down serious attempts at regulation coming from Washington and state capitals. But in cities and towns, it's often a different story.

"Already most Americans feel like the levers of democracy aren't working for them anymore," Mary Bottari of the Center for Media and Democracy, a Wisconsin-based progressive group that has tracked the preemption trend, told me. "Congress's ratings are in the pits, people feel like nothing ever changes. But most people generally feel a lot better about their local government."

Local government is where the voices of ordinary people still stand a chance of being heard, because citizens are much closer to the decision makers, while special interests, no matter how powerful, can't monitor thousands of city or county councils around the country. It's the last remaining place where a key promise of our political system still holds reasonably true: that a motivated, organized group of everyday Americans has a decent shot at exerting influence.

That's why by explicitly looking to take power away from local government, advocates of preemption are undermining not just local democracy but democracy writ large. Indeed, it's perhaps no coincidence that some of the very same elected officials pushing for preemption—Scott Walker and Greg Abbott among them—are also leading the fight to roll back other forms of people power. As attorney general, Abbott waged a years-long court battle for Texas's strict voter ID law. Walker and his fellow Wisconsin Republicans, meanwhile, have gone to the mat for their own voter ID measure as well as other voting restrictions.

As if to underscore the point, as 2016 rolled around, Wisconsin Republicans introduced a new preemption bill, one that would bar local governments from issuing new photo ID cards, and would say explicitly that such IDs can't be used to vote.

For Ellen Bravo, it's no surprise that voter suppression and preemption go hand in hand: "You want to limit *who* can vote. You want to limit what they can vote *for*. You want to expand your power over voting in every way you can."

Chapter 4

RIGGING THE PLAYING FIELD

On December 14, 2012, a gunman walked into a Newtown, Connecticut, elementary school and massacred twenty-six people—twenty of them young children—before turning his high-powered rifle on himself.

In the preceding years, mass shootings had become all-too-frequent events, without prompting action from Washington. But in the case of Newtown—because of the ages of the victims, because of the scale of the carnage, and because of the ease with which the perpetrator had gotten his guns, which were part of a massive cache all bought legally by his mother—there was a pervasive sense that, as President Obama put it not long afterward, "this time is different." As Newtown parents lobbied on Capitol Hill for measures to reduce gun violence, they brought pictures of their murdered children to show lawmakers. "They need to not just look us in the eyes, but look at our children and the lost ones and see those faces, see what's gone, and remember this isn't just about political parties," said Nicole Hockley, whose autistic six-year-old son, Dylan, had been killed. "This isn't just about careers. This is about people. And this is about making change to save people."

By the following April, Congress had responded. Senators Joe Manchin of West Virginia, a Democrat, and Pat Toomey of Pennsylvania, a Republican, offered a bill that called for expanding background checks to all gun show and Internet sales. The measure was far from a panacea, but it would have made it harder for criminals and the mentally ill to access deadly weapons, almost certainly saving lives. Polls showed that around 90 percent of Americans favored expanded background checks—what the *Washington Post* called an "extraordinary level of agreement on a political issue."

Then, unexpectedly, the bill failed to pass the Senate.

In the stunned aftermath, the press and the public searched for explanations. How could a commonsense bipartisan measure—proposed in response to a galvanizing national tragedy and with overwhelming popular support—have come up short? Some chalked it up to the power of the National Rifle Association ("a damning indictment of the strangle-hold special interests have on Washington," Mike Bloomberg called it). Others blamed the four red-state Democrats who had abandoned their party on the vote. Still others said it was Manchin's fault for committing a series of "strategic blunders." The consensus was that this represented, as the *Post* put it, a "stunning collapse" for gun control advocates and a "resounding defeat" for President Obama.

Largely overlooked in the postmortems was the fact that fifty-four senators had voted for the Manchin-Toomey bill, while only forty-six had voted against it. But because Republicans had made clear that they would filibuster almost any significant legislation, the parties had already agreed that the measure, as well as several other gun control proposals considered the same day, had to win sixty votes to overcome such a filibuster. Manchin-Toomey "failed" largely because, despite attracting solid majority support, the bill wasn't able to meet the extraordinarily high bar required of it.

Today's Republicans didn't invent the filibuster, of course. But under Obama, they massively expanded its use. In fact, the unprecedented reliance on the filibuster as a routine obstruction tactic has been just one component in a much broader Republican strategy to stymie the president's agenda and win back power by any means possible. As Representative Kevin McCarthy, now the House majority leader, summed it up at a meeting of top Republicans the night before Obama took office: "If you act like you're the minority, you're going to stay in the minority."

This procedural hardball has been bolstered by a fundamental imbalance in the design of the Senate—a small-state bias that favors the GOP. It, too, played a key role in stopping Manchin-Toomey—and it's only getting worse. Even more important, after a stealth campaign years in the making, Republicans in multiple states have been able to draw district lines to maximize their numbers in the House, giving them a virtual lock on control of the chamber into the next decade. That's guaranteed the party an impregnable base of operations from which to block the agenda not just of President Obama but of future Democratic presidents, too.

What it all amounts to is that Washington is broken. But the reason is not a lack of bipartisanship or a failure to compromise. Rather, thanks to a combination of aggressive Republican tactics and design flaws in the system that increasingly work to the party's advantage, Congress isn't representative of the views of the American people, and the GOP is making it even less so. The result is that both election results and legislative outcomes skew much more conservative than most Americans want. This "democracy deficit" has meant that for much of Obama's presidency, pressing legislation meant to solve genuine problems and supported by a clear majority both of the American people and of their representatives has died in the cradle. And it looks set to allow the GOP to continue to exert enormous influence even during a period when it's unlikely to command a national majority.

IN JANUARY 2009, 1.8 million people gathered on the mall for President Obama's first inauguration—the capital's largest crowd ever, for any reason. That night, while the new president was celebrating with the traditional round of Washington balls, top Republicans were busy elsewhere. Much has been made of the split between the party's establishment and conservative wings, but as the Obama era began, both groups had the same goal. Establishment congressional leaders like Paul Ryan, Eric Cantor, and McCarthy, Tea Party favorites like South Carolina senator Jim DeMint and his Oklahoma colleague Tom Coburn, and party elders like Newt Gingrich and the ubiquitous GOP pollster Frank Luntz all came together at the Caucus Room, a high-end D.C. restaurant, to lay out a battle plan for bringing the new president down.

The Republican Party was then at a low point. After two straight electoral drubbings, it held neither the White House nor either house of Congress, though it had controlled all three just over two years earlier. Attendees at the gathering floated a few tactical gambits, like attacking Tim Geithner, Obama's treasury secretary nominee, over unpaid taxes. But much more important, they agreed on a broader strategy. They didn't put it quite like this, but here's what it amounted to: do everything possible to create gridlock by opposing the president's agenda—especially his efforts to lift the country out of the Great Recession, then in its fourteenth brutal month—then use the resulting dissatisfaction to win back the House in 2010 and the Senate and White House two years later. What Republicans understood was that the president and his party would get the credit for any economic progress and would equally get the blame for continued stagnation. So the path back to power wasn't, as conventional wisdom had it, to listen to the voters and find a middle ground. It was to thwart action at all costs.

That strategy was likely to be particularly effective for Republicans, of course, because most voters would see only that Washington was failing—which would naturally drive them toward the party associated with a distrust of government, even if that party was in fact the one responsible for the failure. As one disillusioned longtime Republican congressional staffer wrote, describing his colleagues' thinking, in a bitter 2011 essay, "By sabotaging the reputation of an institution of government, the party that is programmatically against government would come out the relative winner."

Eight days later the GOP faced the first big test of its new strategy: the vote on Obama's stimulus bill. This was the new president's big chance to jolt the economy out of its rut and do something about surging unemployment, now approaching 8 percent. In the House, not a single Republican voted for the bill, and in the Senate, just three—Susan Collins, Olympia

Snowe, and Arlen Specter, soon to become a Democrat—did so. Joining with the conservative Democrat Ben Nelson and the independent Joe Lieberman, Collins and company made the price of their support major cuts to the bill's scope. (Those five votes wouldn't have been needed, of course—a clear majority would have been fine—were it not for the certainty of a Republican filibuster.)

The result? A final package that came in at $787 billion— far less than what many economists said was needed to spur long-lasting growth and make a real dent in the jobless crisis. Today there's a consensus among experts that the stimulus helped boost the economy, but that the recovery over the next few years would have been much faster and stronger had it been larger. Ordinary Americans likely paid the price: later that year, unemployment rose to 10 percent. But the plan worked well for the GOP: in 2010, with the economy still in the doldrums, Republicans retook the House by an overwhelming margin and cut into Democrats' Senate advantage.

The economy would keep limping along for several years, with little help from Washington. Republicans continued to oppose almost any form of spending that might get things moving. They stood in the way of extending unemployment benefits, one of the most effective policies at spurring growth, not to mention reducing the day-to-day suffering of millions of Americans. They actively created crises over government funding and the national debt in order to force round after round of spending cuts—even though cutting short-term spending during a downturn flew in the face of what almost every mainstream economist was recommending. And all but one Senate Republican voted against even debating a 2014 effort by Senate Democrats to boost the minimum wage.

The 2011 debt ceiling fiasco was perhaps the most illuminating episode. Raising the debt ceiling had until then been a routine piece of congressional housekeeping—it doesn't create new spending, it just authorizes the government to pay creditors for the money Congress has already spent. But Republicans made clear throughout the spring that they'd refuse to raise the ceiling unless Obama agreed to major budget cuts.

The threat carried weight, because if the ceiling wasn't lifted, the United States could potentially default on its debt—which could have thrown the global economy into turmoil just as it was struggling to recover from the Great Recession. Mitch McConnell, the Senate Republican leader, called the debt ceiling "a hostage that's worth ransoming." In the end, Obama blinked, agreeing to a complex package of cuts that ultimately amounted to over $2 trillion over ten years—much of it from the defense budget, but a good chunk from programs like Head Start, special education, and public housing.

The Yale constitutional law professor Jack Balkin has called the debt ceiling standoff "a failed attempt to stage a revolution in American politics with control of only one house of Congress." The revolution may not have materialized, but it's hard not to conclude it was at least a policy victory for the GOP. Speaker John Boehner exulted that he got "98 percent" of what he wanted. Democrats, whose low-income constituents bore the brunt of many of the cuts, were less enthused. Missouri representative Emanuel Cleaver, a Democrat whose district encompasses most of Kansas City, called it a "sugar-coated satan sandwich," adding, "If I were a Republican, this is a night to party."

———

AROUND THE TIME when Ryan, Gingrich, and their allies were plotting at the Caucus Room, a little-known organization called the Republican State Leadership Committee (RSLC) saw an opportunity of its own. The group was dedicated to electing GOP candidates at the state level—but its leaders were thinking bigger. In thirty-seven states, legislatures are in charge of drawing district lines for congressional and state legislative races, based on the once-a-decade census. A new round of redistricting was coming up in 2011. That meant that if Republicans came out of the 2010 elections with control of key state legislatures, they could achieve a twofer: by drawing favorable boundaries, they could not only entrench themselves in power in a slew of state capitals, but they could also rig the U.S. House in their favor for at least a decade. Thus was born the Redistricting Majority Project—it went by the brazen acronym REDMAP—the RSLC's master plan to target state legislative races in order to control the upcoming redistricting process.

Of course, political parties of all stripes have been using the power to draw district lines to benefit their side for at least two centuries. It was the unnatural-looking salamander-shaped districts created in 1812 under Massachusetts governor—and noted democracy skeptic—Elbridge Gerry to boost his Democratic-Republican Party that gave us the term *gerrymander*. But not until the RSLC's REDMAP did a national party focus its political strategy so centrally on anticipating the chance to redistrict to its own advantage, or give it the kind of resources the new initiative would receive.

In early 2010 the RSLC recruited Ed Gillespie, an ultra-connected GOP lobbyist and veteran Beltway political operative, as its top fund-raiser. Armed with a detailed PowerPoint presentation, Gillespie took on the challenging task of convincing Republican donors from Wall Street to Dallas to fund candidates they'd never heard of who were running in obscure state legislative races. At every step he explained that, thanks to the upcoming redistricting, the GOP could use its control of state houses to give itself a massive advantage on the ultimate playing field of the U.S. Congress.

That spring Gillespie flew from Washington to Raleigh, N.C., for lunch with Art Pope, the multimillionaire founder of a chain of discount stores and a major funder of conservative causes. Democrats held majorities in both houses of North Carolina's legislature, but the two men saw an opportunity. Pope, his family members, and groups he controls would ultimately spend $2.2 million, not all of it through REDMAP, on North Carolina's state legislative races that fall—a massive sum for state-level politics. Most of it went to pay for slashing attacks against Democrats. John Snow, a retired judge and conservative Democratic state senator, was subjected to a barrage of Pope-financed hits, a mix of TV ads and mailers that cost several hundred thousand dollars. One mailer went after Snow for "wasting our tax dollars" by voting to spend $218,000 on a Shakespeare festival, without noting that this was actually a budget cut for the program. Another seized on Snow's work on a 2009 state law that aimed to address the huge racial disparity in death penalty cases by allowing judges to reconsider death sentences if there was evidence of racism in the original verdict. Echoing the Willie Horton ad that had helped sink Michael Dukakis, it showed Henry McCollum, an African-American death row inmate, and described in gruesome detail how he and three other men had raped and murdered an eleven-year-old girl. Then it told readers: "Thanks to arrogant State Senator John Snow, Mc-Collum could soon be let off death row." Snow ultimately lost the election to his Republican opponent, an orthodontist with ties to the Tea Party, by fewer than two hundred votes. Other Democrats in the state faced similar attacks. One state assembly candidate, Chris Heagarty, who is white, was depicted in a mailer with a sombrero, next to the message: "Mucho taxo, adios senor!" In the end, it was a rout. Republicans won eighteen of the twenty-two districts that Pope and his groups targeted, gaining eleven seats in the state senate and fifteen in the house, and winning full control of the state legislature for the first time since Reconstruction.[*]

North Carolina wasn't the only state where Gillespie's push paid off. Across the country the RSLC raised $30 million–dwarfing the Democrats' $10 million–most of it spent in a massive post–Labor Day advertising blitz. The money was laser-focused, of course, on certain states where state lawmakers ran the redistricting process and legislative control of one or more chambers was genuinely up for grabs. When the smoke cleared, the GOP, aided by the Tea Party wave that also helped them take the U.S. House, had picked up 675 state legislative seats and flipped 21 state legislative chambers from Democratic to Republican control. More important, they now ran both chambers–and therefore enjoyed a nearly free hand to draw district lines–in twenty-five states, compared to the Dem-

---

[*] After the GOP won the state's governorship, too, in 2012, Pope became North Carolina's top budget official, and helped implement a sweeping lurch to the right that included both the ultrarestrictive 2013 voting law and the further loosening of limits on money in politics.

ocrats' thirteen. Crucially, the GOP's haul included key redistricting battlefields—that is, large states where the legislature was in charge of drawing new districts—like Florida, Pennsylvania, Ohio, Michigan, North Carolina, and Virginia.

Now it was time to reap the benefits. In state houses across the country, Republican legislators hired friendly map-drawing specialists who took advantage of software that was exponentially more sophisticated than a decade ago. Their goal was to allocate Republican voters more efficiently than Democratic ones for the purpose of winning as many seats as possible. That meant many Democratic voters—often urban minorities—were herded into a small number of safe districts, creating a large number of "wasted" Democratic votes. (The mapmakers were helped by the fact that, increasingly, Democrats cluster in denser areas than Republicans, who tend to be more spread out, meaning it's easier to pack Democrats together.) Other Democratic areas were then split into pieces and joined with larger, Republican-leaning areas, creating districts that gave the GOP a leg up. Thanks to a 2004 Supreme Court ruling in which the five conservative justices had held that gerrymandering disputes are political questions and therefore can't even be heard by the courts unless they involve racial discrimination claims, the mapmakers could act with little fear of legal challenges.

The process inevitably produced districts with shapes that rivaled Gerry's salamander. Pennsylvania's seventh district, outside Philadelphia, measured just eight hundred feet across at one point and jumped over the Schuylkill River at another. One independent mapmaker called it a "monstrosity—certain to be a poster-child for future gerrymandering studies."

More damaging than the odd shapes was the way neighborhoods were broken up to ensure their Democratic residents didn't constitute a majority. That violated a basic good-government principle, often reflected in state law, that districts should as much as possible constitute what political mapmakers call "communities of interest." That is, they should strive not to split up cohesive communities, or to force together areas with different interests, so as to allow for representation that best aligns with a community's needs.

One egregious example came from Texas. In an email, Eric Opiela, a Republican state legislative staffer, asked one of the mapmakers hired by the GOP for help in "shoring up" an incumbent Tea Party Republican congressman, Quico Canseco, in District 23. Canseco and the GOP were popular with white voters in the district, but Hispanic voters favored Democrats. But if Republicans had simply removed Hispanic voters from the district, they would have risked running afoul of the Voting Rights Act, which bars racially motivated gerrymanders. So instead, Opiela suggested removing Hispanic areas with high voter turnout and replacing them with ones with low turnout—thereby keeping the district's share of Hispanics roughly the same while still making it much more GOP-friendly. The result was a map that split the heavily Hispanic border town of Eagle Pass right down Main Street, pulling the high turnout neighborhood out of Canseco's district. "For anybody in Eagle Pass, if you told them it was two different congressional districts, it would completely baffle them," said Michael Li, an election lawyer who closely followed Texas's redistricting process.

The old lines for District 23 were ultimately restored by a federal court as part of a challenge to the state's redistricting process under the Voting Rights Act, and Canseco was ousted in 2012 by Democrat Pete Gallego.[*] But for the most part, the GOP's gerrymander plan worked beautifully, as became clear on Election Day 2012. In four large states—Michigan, North Carolina, Pennsylvania, and Wisconsin—Democratic House candidates got more votes, yet Republicans won more seats.[**] The skew was most egregious in Pennsylvania, where 48.8 percent of the vote for Republicans translated into thirteen of the state's eighteen congressional seats, or over 72 percent. In each of the four states, the RSLC had spent $1 million or close to it to win control in 2010—a huge sum for state-level races, which typically don't involve TV ads. In several other states, including Florida, Virginia, and Ohio, Republicans won significantly more seats in 2012 than their share of votes deserved—in Ohio, for instance, 55 percent of the vote for the GOP translated into 75 percent of the seats. But perhaps the starkest numbers were the national ones. Democratic House candidates won about 1.4 million more votes than Republicans, but the GOP came away with a thirty-three-seat advantage—just the second time since World War II that the party with fewer votes won a majority.

"There is no question—none—that the recent redistricting effort distorted the vote," Ken Mayer, a political science professor at the University of Wisconsin–Madison said at the time, referring to his state's experience. "Nobody takes seriously the

---

[*] Republicans won the seat back in a close race in 2014. In a stark example of how different prongs of the GOP's push to undermine democracy can reinforce one another, this was the race that might have been determined by Texas's strict voter ID law.

[**] In Arizona, the reverse was true: Democrats got fewer votes but more seats. But an independent commission had drawn Arizona's districts.

notion that the legislative plan for congressional districts wasn't politically motivated." The following January, in an unusually candid report on REDMAP's success, the RSLC took a victory lap. "The rationale was straightforward," the report read. "Controlling the redistricting process in these states would have the greatest impact in determining how both state legislative and congressional district boundaries would be drawn."

North Carolina Republicans were even more brazen. In February 2016, just weeks before the state's primary, a federal court ruled the state's map, which was created by the RNC's longtime redistricting expert, to be an unconstitutional racial gerrymander. The court said one "serpentine" congressional district was "contorted and contrived" to pack in African-American voters. GOP lawmakers were unfazed. They quickly set about drawing a new map that would still advantage their party, only without using race as a factor. "Our intent is to use the political data we have to our partisan advantage," one Republican legislator testified. "I acknowledge freely that this would be a political gerrymander, which is not against the law." One Democrat could barely contain his outrage. "They have no shame about it," he told a reporter. "They've drawn a supermajority for themselves, and that's not a democracy."

The striking success of the GOP's scheme would permanently change the redistricting game. This time around both parties are starting early and aiming much bigger: REDMAP says it plans to take in $125 million for the 2020 state races, which will determine who draws the next round of maps. A competing Democratic super PAC has set a goal of $70 million. REDMAP's success last time "really helped redefine how the American political system looks at the redistricting process," RSLC director Matt Walter said last year.

More important, it has all but ensured a Republican-led House at least until 2022. What would Democrats need to do to win back the House under the current districts? According to projections made by the good-government group FairVote, they'd have to win ten million more votes than Republicans— better than a 55–45 margin. That all but guarantees that even if a Democrat wins the next presidential election, Republicans will still exercise an effective veto in the House for years to come.

BUT IF THE House is fixed for Republicans at least into the next decade, the Senate's rightward slant may be even more permanent.

One driver is the structure of the chamber itself. Because each state elects two senators, regardless of population, Americans from smaller states get much more representation than those from larger ones. This setup has worked against democracy from the start, but it's become much more damaging of late, when a state's size and its political outlook are increasingly likely to be correlated. The other driver is more pernicious: a concerted Republican strategy of using the Senate's many checks on majority rule to paralyze the chamber and make it as difficult as possible for the elected president to govern.

Many Americans, especially defenders of the status quo, assume that both the small-state bias and the filibuster reflect high-minded principles like state sovereignty and the protection of minority rights. In fact, both are pure accidents of history.

It's true that some of the Founders saw the Senate as representing not the people but the states as individual sovereign actors. But what really carried the day was that small states, worried about being dominated by their larger neighbors, insisted on the principle of equal representation for states as a condition of their willingness to sign on to the whole enterprise. Madison argued vociferously against the idea but ultimately came around so as not to risk torpedoing the emerging union. Connecticut's Roger Sherman proposed the structure that became enshrined in the Constitution—a bicameral legislature with a House of Representatives reflecting the population and a Senate equally apportioned among the states—an arrangement that has become known as the Connecticut Compromise.

The Senate's setup, in other words, was the result of some effective political hardball by small states. Just how hard? While other parts of the Constitution can be changed with the support of two-thirds of each House and three-quarters of the states, the Senate's equal-representation-of-states principle can't be undone without the unanimous agreement of the states—something that's likely to remain a nonstarter pretty much forever, since why would small states voluntarily give up their power?

Even at the Founding, this setup created a stark imbalance in representation. Virginia, then the largest state, had roughly twelve times as many people as Delaware, the smallest. But since then the difference has exploded. Today California, with a population of nearly 39 million people, is roughly sixty-six times as large as Wyoming, population 584,000—meaning a Californian has only one-sixty-sixth the amount of representation in the Senate as a Wyomingite. Or think of it this way: A majority of Americans now live in just nine states. That majority has eighteen votes in the Senate, while the minority has eighty-two.

These differences have real effects on policy outcomes. In 2013 the *New York Times* compared Rutland County, Vermont, to Washington County, New York, which sits just across the state border. It found that Rutland received four times as much money from the stimulus bill, even though the two counties are almost exactly the same size. Rutland used the money to fund roads and preschool programs—even its fish population got help, via a program to ensure that a project to rebuild a bridge didn't affect piscine life. As for Washington County, "we never saw any of the positive impact of the stimulus funds," a local chamber of commerce official told the paper. Why the difference? In large part, the *Times* concluded, because New York has thirty times as many people as Vermont, giving Vermonters thirty times the level of Senate representation. While New York's two senators had to spread their efforts to get stimulus money among nineteen million people, Vermont's only had 625,000 to worry about.

The effect of the imbalance isn't random. Because larger states tend to be much more urban than smaller ones (there are exceptions, of course—think of small, urban Rhode Island), the preferences of city dwellers get far less consideration in the Senate than those of rural Americans—a reality underscored by the continued existence of needless agricultural subsidies. Many of Obamacare's details were hammered out by a self-appointed council of six self-proclaimed moderate senators who collectively represented just 6.5 million predominantly rural people from Montana, Wyoming, North Dakota, Iowa, New Mexico, and Maine—less than 3 percent of the total U.S. population, and fewer than the population of New York City.

The Senate's overrepresentation of rural interests has racial implications, too. Nonwhites make up 44 percent of the population in the ten largest states, but just 18 percent in the ten smallest, giving whites far more weight in the Senate than their numbers deserve. Perhaps that's one reason (the cost of today's statewide campaigns is another) why only six out of one hundred senators are nonwhite, compared to 37 percent of the U.S. population. That's up from just three in 2001. It doesn't help that Washington, D.C., which is nearly 50 percent black and is more populous than both Wyoming and Vermont, has zero senators—thanks in part to continued opposition by congressional Republicans to giving the district's roughly 650,000 residents any real representation in Congress at all.

But even if race weren't a factor, the partisan divide would remain—and worsen. It's now easier than ever for Americans to pick up and move, and people's political views are increasingly aligned with their cultural and lifestyle choices. As a result, over the last few decades, we've sorted ourselves into like-minded— and like-voting—communities. At the most basic level, urban areas are becoming ever more Democratic, and rural ones ever more Republican. Because urban states tend to be more populous than rural ones, Republican senators are more likely to come from small states, and Democratic senators from big ones. That imbalance gives the GOP a major leg up in the fight for control of the Senate: even though Republican senators received twenty million fewer votes than did Democrats and the independents who caucus with them, Republicans hold a 54–46 majority.

It also tilts legislative outcomes. One study found that between 1990 and 2010, 10 percent of major votes in the Senate would have come out differently had states been represented according to their size. In 24 of 27 such votes, Republicans benefited. The Manchin-Toomey gun control vote perfectly illustrated the point. Among the 25 largest states, the measure got 33 yes votes and 17 no votes. But among the 25 smallest, it got just 21 yes votes and 29 no. The 54 senators who voted for the bill represented 62 percent of Americans—meaning that if states were represented in the Senate in proportion to their populations, the bill would even have passed the 60 percent threshold needed to overcome a filibuster. A separate gun control measure offered that day by Senator Dianne Feinstein, which would have regulated assault weapons, got just 40 votes. But its supporters represented 52 percent of the population, meaning it too would have passed if the Senate were organized democratically.

As if small states weren't favored enough, research suggests that their senators have more often taken advantage of another of the Senate's antidemocratic features: the filibuster.

If the Senate itself was a child of compromise, the filibuster was created entirely by accident. Originally the Senate, like the House, had a rule known as the "previous question motion," which allowed a simple majority to cut off debate and move to a vote. But in 1805 Aaron Burr—not long after killing Alexander Hamilton in their famous duel—was presiding over the Senate in his capacity as vice president and decided that the chamber had too many duplicative rules. Burr urged senators to scrap some of them, including the previous question motion. The rule wasn't well understood at the time, and so the following year it was dropped from the Senate rulebook. But apparently by oversight, senators didn't create any other way to restrict debate. "We say the Senate developed the filibuster to protect minorities and the right to debate," Sarah Binder, an expert on congressional procedure at the Brookings Institution, has said. "That's hogwash! It's a mistake. Believe me, I would've loved to find the smoking gun where the Senate decides to create a deliberative body. But it takes years before anyone figures out that the filibuster has just been created."

Indeed, the first filibuster didn't take place until an 1837 dispute between supporters and opponents of President Andrew Jackson—and it was hardly an example of high-minded deliberation. Three years earlier the Senate's Whig majority had formally censured Jackson as part of an investigation into his effort to defund the Bank of the United States, which had supported his political opponents. Now, after an influx of pro-Jackson Democrats, legislation was offered to expunge the censure. To block the measure, the Whigs just kept talking. "It was evident that consumption of time, delay and adjournment, was their plan," Senator Thomas Benton, a Missouri Democrat, later wrote. He and his fellow Jackson supporters, Benton added, readied to stick around all night "fortif[ying] themselves with an ample supply, ready in a nearby committee room, of cold hams, turkeys, beef, pickles, wines, and cups of hot coffee." In the end, the Whigs gave in, and the legislation passed.

Filibusters became more common in the decades that followed, but despite various attempts at reform, it wasn't until 1917 that a cloture rule was added to provide a means of cutting debate short. The move was triggered when eleven isolationist senators drew nationwide scorn for filibustering a White House–backed bill to arm American merchant ships in response to German aggression in the North Atlantic during the run-up to the U.S. entry into World War I. The "Senate of the United States," thundered President Woodrow Wilson, in a broadside that rings remarkably true a century later, "is the only legislative body in the world which cannot act when its majority is ready for action.

A little group of willful men, representing no opinion but their own, have rendered the great government of the United States helpless and contemptible. . . . The only remedy is that the rules of the Senate should be so altered that it can act."

But fatefully, the new rules still required that two-thirds of senators support any motion to end debate. (In 1975, after several failed attempts, the two-thirds requirement would be reduced to three-fifths, or sixty votes.) Supporters of segregation took advantage of the filibuster to block antilynching bills in the 1920s, anti-poll-tax bills in the 1930s and '40s, and numerous other antidiscrimination measures for decades after the Second World War. The 1957 Civil Rights Act triggered the longest individual speech the Senate has ever seen, a twenty-four-hour-plus ode to states' rights given by South Carolina's Strom Thurmond, at the time a Democrat. (The senator quit only after his doctor expressed concern about possible kidney damage.)

Still, as harmful and undemocratic as they were, these segregationist filibusters were understood, especially by their participants, not as routine obstruction tactics but as extreme measures in response to far-reaching legislation that could change the face of southern life. Even during the turbulent 1960s, only about thirty cloture motions—that is, motions to cut off debate, a good indicator that a filibuster is happening or threatened—were filed in total throughout the decade.

As the parties became more ideologically cohesive starting in the 1970s, the use of the filibuster grew. At first, the change was gradual. There are various ways to measure filibusters, but if we're interested in their use to block the governing agenda of the opposing party, we need to focus on the periods when the Senate and the White House were both held by the same party.

In the six years from the start of 1963 to the end of 1968, when Presidents John Kennedy and Lyndon Johnson were in office, throughout which Democrats held the Senate, there were only seventeen cloture motions. The rate gradually went up under Carter and Reagan, until it reached 130 during the four full years of President George W. Bush's tenure that Republicans controlled the Senate, from 2003 to 2006.

So when Obama took office in 2009 with large majorities in both houses, the use of the filibuster was already in the midst of a four-decade-long rise. But that's when it exploded. During the six years when Democrats controlled the Senate under Obama, there were 505 cloture votes, over twice the rate that the Republican majority under Bush faced. Perhaps even more unprecedented was the routine filibustering of Obama's judicial and executive branch nominees—previously an area where presidents have enjoyed broad leeway. A deal in late 2013 ended that practice, though not for Supreme Court nominees. But in the five years of Obama's presidency when it existed, there were eighty-one motions to end such filibusters, compared to thirty-eight during Bush's six years with a Republican Senate.

The GOP's use of the filibuster under Obama didn't just offend abstract principles like majority rule—it also meant that pressing real-world needs went unmet. Among the pieces of major legislation that would have likely become law were it not for the filibuster was a bill that would have provided a public option as part of Obamacare. Another casualty was a measure that would have required corporations to disclose their political spending, in response to the *Citizens United* ruling. A third would have required states to provide collective bargaining rights to police and firefighters. And a fourth would have made it easier for women to raise concerns about pay inequality in the workplace—that one received fifty-eight votes but still failed.

Indeed, by early 2016, Senate Republicans had made such a habit of violating long-standing constitutional norms that perhaps their most consequential act of sabotage surprised almost no one in Washington. Within hours of the news that Justice Scalia had died, McConnell announced that the Senate simply would refuse to act on any replacement Obama might nominate, even though the president had nearly a year left in office. McConnell offered no real justification for creating a year-long vacancy on the nation's highest court. He said only that "the American people should have a voice" in the selection of the next justice—as if President Obama had not himself been elected by the American people.

And yet, the GOP's very refusal to act was perhaps the best illustration yet of how its extreme tactics have been driven by desperation. An Obama nominee would likely create a liberal majority on the court for the first time in nearly half a century— the result of Democrats holding the White House for sixteen of the last twenty-four years. Conservatives feared that if that happened, progressive rulings on climate change, government power, abortion, affirmative action, voting, money in politics, and more could transform the country. As The New Yorker's Jeffrey Toobin wrote the day after Scalia was buried, "This Republican intransigence is a sign of panic, not power."

OF COURSE, WHAT'S an opposition party to do, if not oppose the president? If Republican leaders genuinely believed the policies advanced by Obama and the Democrats would hurt the country, they were right to do everything they could to stop them. Despite what some Beltway pundits seem to believe, bipartisanship is no end in itself.

But the GOP's opposition to Obama has been characterized by an unprecedented level of coordination, discipline, and policy cynicism. As we've seen, it has at every stage relied on reducing the level of democracy on offer. And in doing so, it has worsened a genuine structural crisis that threatens to all but paralyze our system of government.

For much of the twentieth century, the parties were loose coalitions of interests: The Democratic Party, for instance, included both northern working-class ethnics and southern segregationists. That meant that even during times of divided government, it was sometimes possible to get things done, because interparty alliances were common. Today political scientists describe the parties—especially the GOP—as far more cohesive, parliamentary-style units, giving them much less incentive to work with one another. Throw in the rise of the filibuster—itself a product of this increased party cohesion—and you have a situation that's pretty much untenable for a working democracy: with few exceptions, in order to enact almost any far-reaching legislation, a party must simultaneously hold the White House, the House of Representatives, and a sixty-seat majority in the Senate.

That, of course, almost never happens. But for the blink of an eye during Obama's presidency, it did. In July 2009 Senator Al Franken of Minnesota took office after the protracted court battle that followed his razor-thin 2008 victory over Norm Coleman. (Indeed, Republicans drew out the legal dispute in order to deny Democrats their sixtieth vote.) But Ted Kennedy's illness had already left him housebound by the time Franken arrived, and after Kennedy's death that summer, his temporary Democratic replacement wasn't sworn in until late September. That meant the Democrats didn't have an effective sixtieth vote until then. In February 2010 Scott Brown took office after winning a special election in Massachusetts to replace Kennedy permanently, ending the Democrats' supermajority. Throw in the holiday recess, and Democrats had a genuine filibuster-proof majority for only about fourteen weeks.

It's no accident that this brief interlude saw the passage in the Senate of the most important measure enacted under Obama—the Affordable Care Act, which received no GOP votes. In fact, after Brown's victory cost Democrats their sixtieth Senate vote, the threat of a filibuster forced the House to simply pass an amended version of the Senate's bill, to avoid another Senate vote. That unusual process led to flaws in the bill's drafting, which in turn opened the door to Republican-backed lawsuits.

Obamacare aside, this is no way to run a country. Even in a perfectly fair election system, these intervals of one-party control, with sixty votes in the Senate, would be rare indeed. But thanks to in-built Republican advantages across the board, which are getting worse, they figure to come around for Democrats perhaps once every few decades at most. In other words, if nothing changes, you can expect the next opportunity for Washington to produce transformative progressive legislation to come sometime around 2040.

Chapter 5

THE NEW JUDICIAL ACTIVISM

Washington's Mayflower Hotel, a stone's throw from the White House, has been a witness to history both high-flown and tawdry. President Franklin Roosevelt wrote his first inaugural, delivered during the depths of the Great Depression—"the only thing we have to fear is . . . fear itself"—in Room 776. J. Edgar Hoover ate chicken soup for lunch in the hotel's dining room nearly every day for twenty years. Republican members of Congress pushing for the impeachment of Bill Clinton grilled Monica Lewinsky in the presidential suite. And it was there that Eliot Spitzer and Ashley Dupré had the $4,300 tryst that would end his tenure as New York's governor. President Harry Truman called the hotel "Washington's second-best address."

In November 2009, less than a year into Obama's first term, the Mayflower hosted the annual convention of the Federalist Society, the hugely influential organization of conservative lawyers whose membership list has included Antonin Scalia, Clarence Thomas, Sam Alito, and Ken Starr, among others. According to one history of the group, every federal judge appointed by the two presidents Bush was either a member of the

Federalist Society or was approved by White House staffers who were. The convention offers a chance for the leading lights of the conservative legal world and those who want to join their ranks to network and to trade ideas for advancing their grand project, under way since the 1970s: moving the law to the right. That year the roughly one thousand attendees heard speeches by a list of conservative luminaries from Alito to Senator Jeff Sessions, the former Alabama attorney general who has become Donald Trump's top foreign policy adviser. A panel discussion on "redistribution of wealth" featured Steve Forbes, the publishing heir and two-time Republican presidential candidate with an estimated net worth of over $430 million.

Still, not everyone found all the panels scintillating. During an exploration of "Bailouts and Government as Insurer of Last Resort," a few attendees decamped to chat in the hall. Among them were Todd Gaziano, who ran the legal program for the Heritage Foundation, and Randy Barnett, a Georgetown Law professor who's prominent in conservative and libertarian legal circles.

"Hey, Randy, do you have any thoughts about the constitutionality of the health care law?" Gaziano asked, referring to the Affordable Care Act.

"You know, I really haven't given it much thought," Barnett replied.

That week the Democratic-controlled House had narrowly passed a version of the sweeping health care legislation that represented the centerpiece of the president's domestic agenda, but it was still awaiting a vote in the Senate. Up to that point, most conservative attacks on the law had just claimed it was disastrous policy. Sarah Palin was screaming about death panels and rationing of care. Republican lawmakers were warning it would throw the insurance market into turmoil, causing people to lose coverage they liked. Tea Party activists called it tyranny. But a few months earlier, two former Justice Department lawyers from the Reagan administration, David Rivkin and Lee Casey, had published op-eds in the *Washington Post* and *Wall Street Journal* making a very different and more sophisticated argument: that the bill's requirement that all Americans buy health insurance or pay a fine, a provision known as the individual mandate, was "profoundly unconstitutional" because it violated the limits on what the federal government can regulate under the Commerce Clause. The argument struck at the heart of the law: if the mandate were knocked out by the courts, the whole thing could well self-destruct. Without it, there would be no way to bring in the younger, healthier people whose participation was needed to offset the older, sicker population and create a viable insurance market. At the very least, the law would work far less efficiently.

Gaziano thought Rivkin and Casey might be on to something, and he wanted to get Barnett on board. If conservatives failed to stop the law through the legislative process—and Democratic majorities in both houses suggested that was likely—the Supreme Court could yet come to their rescue. Gaziano's plan was to quickly draft a report offering a basis for constitutional challenges to the law, then share it with friendly GOP lawmakers. After a bit of cajoling, Barnett agreed to help.

The report that Gaziano, Barnett, and a few others produced several weeks later, "Why the Personal Mandate to Buy Health Insurance Is Unprecedented and Unconstitutional," would help launch a legal challenge to Obamacare that came within one vote of taking down the president's most significant accomplishment. But it would also exemplify an uncompromising and far-reaching new legal strategy that has emerged in the Obama era among opponents of the president's agenda—especially those with small-government, libertarian leanings.

It's an approach that has effectively turned conservative thinking about the role of the courts on its head. For much of the twentieth century and into the twenty-first, the right stressed the need for judges to act with restraint and to defer to democratically elected lawmakers. Conservatives, from senators to the rank-and-file, routinely warned of the dangers of "judicial activism," in which liberal judges read the Constitution expansively to find new rights, as in *Roe v. Wade* or *Griswold v. Connecticut,* the 1965 ruling in which the Supreme Court identified a right to privacy. But in recent years, as conservatives have found it more difficult to make progress in the conventional way—by winning elections—they increasingly have sought to sidestep the political process by urging the same unelected judges whose influence they once decried to rein in legislative majorities. All of a sudden activist judges are the last line of defense against the mob.

FOR NEARLY a century, most conservative judges, and even some liberal ones, have preached the importance of judicial restraint. That's the idea that judges should give the benefit of the doubt to the elected branches of government, since only those branches are accountable to the people. But proponents of the new judicial activism, which many of them prefer to call "judicial engagement," take the opposite view. They say judges should avoid tipping the scales in favor of legislatures and shouldn't hesitate to strike down laws if they find them to violate the Constitution. In a nutshell, judicial engagement advocates explicitly aim to reduce the deference that judges customarily give to the democratic process.

Even though we've long seen conservatives wring their hands about unelected judges legislating from the bench, the notion that judges should strike down *more* laws, not fewer, in fact has deep historical roots on the right. As the legal writer Ian Millhiser has shown, "for much of the period between the Civil War and the New Deal, Supreme Court litigation was the most powerful tool in the right-wing arsenal, a weapon that could sweep aside the collective will of the American people based on the command of just five men in robes." Proponents of this approach often proudly perceived themselves to be acting explicitly in opposition to democratic values, and their rhetoric was in sync with the broader backlash to democracy that took shape during the late nineteenth century. Thanks to the "growth and development of universal suffrage," which lets the masses "enforce their views of civil polity upon the civilized world," Christopher Tiedeman, a conservative legal scholar who was one of the foremost advocates of this early judicial activism, wrote in 1886, "the conservative classes stand in constant fear of the advent of an absolutism more tyrannical and more unreasoning than any before experienced by man—the absolutism of a democratic majority."

This era saw the development of a conservative jurisprudence based on the view that the Constitution bars the government from taking a wide range of steps aimed at regulating businesses or transferring wealth. In one 1895 case Justice Stephen Field called an income tax passed the previous year and affecting less than 10 percent of households an "assault upon capital" that would lead to "a war of the poor against the rich, a war constantly growing in intensity and bitterness." (Only with the ratification of the Sixteenth Amendment in 1913 would a federal income tax become viable.) In 1905 the Court held in the landmark *Lochner v. New York* case that the due process clause of the Fourteenth Amendment to the Constitution provides for a "right of contract" between employers and employees and therefore bars almost any attempt to regulate issues pertaining to that relationship. *Lochner,* which is often taught in law schools today as an example of what judges shouldn't do, ushered in an era in which the Supreme Court consistently struck down legislation passed by Congress and state governments to boost pay or improve conditions for workers. These measures were often aimed primarily at helping easily exploited women and children—who, although lacking a right to vote, were nonetheless seen as enjoying a right to contract that superseded any efforts to pass laws that helped them.

This conservative judicial activism reached its nadir during the New Deal era. First, in 1935 the Supreme Court struck down the law creating the National Recovery Administration, the cornerstone of President Franklin Roosevelt's plan to drag American industry out of the Great Depression. The following year the Court nixed the Agricultural Adjustment Act, created to rescue the struggling, drought-plagued farming sector. Both rulings rested on a strikingly narrow interpretation of what counts as economic activity under the Commerce Clause. Even coal mining—a vast industry stretching from Montana to Pennsylvania—did not qualify as interstate commerce, according to another ruling, putting it, too, beyond the reach of regulation by Congress. Months later, citing *Lochner,* the court struck down a New York minimum wage law, saying the government could do nothing to stop a Brooklyn laundry owner from exploiting his female employees.

In striking down the New Deal agencies, the Court recognized that Roosevelt and Congress were acting with strong public support to ameliorate a once-in-a-century economic cataclysm. But, it said, that didn't matter. "Extraordinary conditions do not create or enlarge constitutional powers," wrote Chief Justice Charles Evans Hughes in the National Recovery Administration case. Only after Roosevelt controversially tried to persuade Congress to let him replace some justices did the Court adopt a broader interpretation of the government's authority under the Constitution, upholding the laws that created Social Security and the National Labor Relations Board.

After that, things shifted massively. In the 1938 *U.S. v. Carolene Products* case, the Supreme Court confirmed that economic regulations passed by Congress don't require close scrutiny by the courts. More important, a footnote in the decision, written by Justice Harlan Stone, attempted to spell out just when the Court *should* intervene. After all, even the most ardent democrat believes that some rights should be protected from elected majorities. The issue is to define which ones. According to Stone, laws that dealt with "the very essence of ordered liberty" deserved closer scrutiny from the Court. That meant, for obvious reasons, laws that stymie the political process through which they might have been repealed, as well as laws "against discrete and insular minorities" who are victims of "prejudice." The University of Chicago scholar David Strauss has called Stone's footnote "the Court's first—and maybe only—attempt to say, systematically, when the courts should declare laws unconstitutional."

The *Carolene Products* footnote provided the basis for much of the Supreme Court's agenda in the decades that followed, when it struck down school segregation measures, poll taxes, limits on free speech, and more. And it remains a pretty good guide to what most modern liberals believe about when courts should intervene. In a 2013 speech Justice Ruth Bader Ginsburg said that in general "we trust the democratic process, so the court is highly deferential to what Congress does," but that laws of the kind described in the *Carolene Products* footnote deserve much closer scrutiny.

For fifty years or so, the liberal judicial activism of the Court, strongest in the 1950s and '60s, turned conservatives into ardent defenders of the sanctity of the popular will. Denouncing unaccountable judges for legislating from the bench became a reliable applause line on the right and remains so today. "Many of our politicians have surrendered to the false god of judicial supremacy, which would allow black-robed and unelected judges the power to make law as well as enforce it," Mike Huckabee declared in 2015.

But that rhetoric belies what's actually going on. The energy on the right is shifting toward the idea that judges should be more, not less, active in striking down laws that they believe violate the Constitution. Barnett, the driving force behind the Obamacare challenge, has been perhaps the single most important figure in building the intellectual architecture that underlies the movement. "What we reject is judges closing their eyes . . . so they may 'defer' to legislative will and uphold legislation without assessing whether the legislation is properly within the power of Congress or state legislatures to enact," he wrote in 2014.

More assertive judges are just a means to an end, of course. The goal is winning stronger protection for the economic rights—primarily property rights and the right of employers and employees to enter into contracts—that nineteenth-century conservatives like Tiedeman and Field believed the Constitution to guarantee. It's not that most courts currently recognize no economic rights, proponents of judicial engagement say. It's that they don't assign them the importance of other rights, like, say, free speech.

"Under current doctrine, the Supreme Court divides your constitutional rights into two categories: meaningful and meaningless," said Clark Neily, a lawyer with the Charles Koch–funded Institute for Justice (IJ), which has led the way in pushing judicial engagement into the mainstream. "Meaningful rights get some form of what the courts call heightened scrutiny, which is simply a euphemism for real. And meaningless rights, like the right to earn a living or own property, get meaningless scrutiny"—that is, there's a lower bar for when those rights can be infringed upon. "In essence what we're asking the court to do is abandon that untenable and artificial distinction."

Many proponents of judicial engagement cheerfully acknowledge that treating economic rights as "meaningful" would make it easier to strike down laws that take almost any significant steps to regulate business or protect workers, potentially returning us to a world before the modern welfare state. Richard Epstein, the libertarian-leaning University of Chicago law professor whose work provides a foundation for much of the judicial engagement school, once admitted, "It will be said that my position invalidates much of the twentieth-century legislation, and so it does. But does that make the position wrong in principle?" In other words, the Constitution prohibits minimum wage laws, health and safety protections for workers, measures barring employment discrimination, and much more.

But leave aside for a moment the frightening real-world effects. What's striking about the push for judicial engagement is how casually it seeks to vastly expand the areas of life that are beyond the reach of the democratic process. In 2011 IJ launched the Center for Judicial Engagement, an internal arm headed by Neily and dedicated exclusively to bringing cases that aim to get courts to enforce economic and property rights. "Government actions are not entitled to 'deference' simply because they result from a political process involving elected representatives," the center declares in its mission statement, adding, "It is the courts' job to check forbidden political impulses, not ratify them under the banner of majoritarian democracy."

Modern proponents of judicial engagement say there's no need to worry that expanding the authority of unelected judges to strike down laws passed by majorities threatens democracy. For one thing, they say, that's what the Founders intended. "The Constitution itself blocks a certain amount of popular will, and it was designed to do that," Neily, a genial libertarian, told me.

In any case, who can say what the popular will really is? "In practice, the claim that laws and administrative regulations reflect the will of the public is often a fiction," Barnett has written, since people tend to know little about them. That's true as far as it goes, of course, but it seems to question the entire concept of representative democracy. People don't have to understand every law passed by government for those laws to have democratic legitimacy—they just need to have elected the people who put them in place.

Finally, proponents of judicial activism say, the Constitution, too, was ratified by a popular majority. So when judges strike down laws, all they're doing is blocking a contemporary majority in the name of an earlier one (which, of course, happened to be made up exclusively of white male property owners).

But if people like Barnett and Neily believe that the courts should be less deferential to the democratic process, Suzanna Sherry goes further. In a 2013 essay that she described as "a rhetorical call to arms and an embrace of judicial activism," Sherry, a law professor at Vanderbilt University, echoed centuries of conservative democracy skeptics, arguing that only by aggressively checking the popular will could the courts avert disaster at the hands of the masses. The paper caused such a splash in libertarian legal circles that Epstein and others participated in a "mini-symposium" to celebrate it. "Too much of a good thing can be bad, and democracy is no exception," Sherry wrote. "The courts should stand in the way of democratic majorities, in order to keep majority rule from degenerating into majority tyranny. . . .

"When the Court fails to act—instead deferring to the elected branches," she concluded, "it abdicates its role as guardian of enduring principles against the temporary passions and prejudices of popular majorities."

In a sign of the progress the judicial engagement crowd has made, Barnett and J. Harvie Wilkinson, a conservative federal appeals court judge and proponent of judicial restraint, sparred over the question of whether courts are too deferential to legislatures. At a sold-out debate held at the Federalist Society's 2013 annual meeting, Barnett declared from the stage, "The sovereignty of the people is not a sovereignty of the majority of the people. Sometimes a majority can act contrary to . . . the general welfare of the community at large."

Barnett's growing rock-star status among right-leaning law students also attests to the shift in attitude. "The younger people, the people in law school, they seem to be gravitating toward people like Randy," Josh Blackman, a conservative law professor and another important player in judicial engagement circles, told the *New Republic* magazine. "When he gets off the stage he's mobbed. . . . There's a crowd of people five or six feet deep surrounding him."

The movement is scoring real-world victories, too. In January 2016 Arizona's Republican governor announced the appointment to the state supreme court of IJ's cofounder, Clint Bolick. Even the old guard is getting on board. Back in 1996 George Will, a reliable weathervane for movement conservatism, at least on domestic issues, condemned "judicial imperialism," lamenting that "democracy is so debilitated" that Americans don't seem to care about judges making decisions for them. These days Will is less worried about democracy. In a 2014 column headlined "Judicial Activism Isn't a Bad Thing," Will criticized judges who "in practicing what conservatives have unwisely celebrated as 'judicial restraint,' have subordinated liberty to majority rule."

THE CHALLENGE TO Obamacare's individual mandate that was hatched at the Mayflower Hotel was a perfect way to get these ideas before the Supreme Court. And because it would potentially destroy President Obama's most important domestic achievement, the architects of the lawsuit knew they could count on full-blooded support from the entire Republican Party. The case would ultimately fail. But just as *Roe v. Wade* helped spur a generation of antiabortion activists, the way in which the mandate was upheld would vastly strengthen those who had sought to defeat it.

Gaziano and Barnett's how-to guide for challenging the mandate was quickly embraced by Republicans. Senator Orrin Hatch had it read into the *Congressional Record,* bolstering its standing as an authoritative text that could be cited in legal documents. Within months, numerous Republican state attorneys general had filed lawsuits relying on Gaziano and Barnett's reasoning.

Most legal observers gave the challenge little chance of success. After all, in *Gonzales v. Raich,* in 2005, the Supreme Court had ruled by a vote of 6–3 that Congress could criminalize the personal medicinal use of homegrown marijuana, even in a state, California, that had legalized medical marijuana. That ruling was controversial, but it rested on what the justices called the "likelihood that the high demand in the interstate market will draw [homegrown] marijuana into that market," making it impossible to draw a clear line between personal use and interstate commerce. (Barnett had argued that case unsuccessfully before the justices.) If homegrown marijuana counted as interstate commerce, surely the vast national health insurance market did, too. But the plaintiffs got around that precedent with a clever argument endorsed by Gaziano and Barnett, and before them Rivkin and Casey: that requiring people to buy insurance regulated not activity but *in*activity. That, they claimed, was unprecedented and not covered under the Commerce Clause.

Just as important, several different suits were filed against the mandate, many in conservative-leaning district courts, so as to boost the odds that at least a few judges ruled against it—a common tactic used by those who push activist lawsuits. In January 2011 Florida district court judge Roger Vinson found for the plaintiffs in a decision that Barnett praised as "extremely deep in its discussion of principles and constitutional doctrine." In fact, Vinson said the mandate was so inextricably tied to the law itself that the whole thing had to be scrapped. Later that year a federal appeals court affirmed most of Vinson's ruling, though it said the rest of the law could limp on without the mandate. But months earlier a different appeals court had upheld the mandate's constitutionality. That created a split that could be resolved only by the Supreme Court.

We all know what happened next. Chief Justice John Roberts, reportedly after having a last-minute change of heart, sided with the four liberal justices to save the Affordable Care Act. Roberts agreed with the plaintiffs that Congress couldn't regulate inactivity. But to rescue the law, he accepted an argument made by the government that the mandate, which requires anyone without health insurance to pay a fine, was actually a tax, which meant Commerce Clause limits didn't apply. In other words, Roberts made clear that he lined up with Barnett and company on the key constitutional question of what Congress can regulate under the Commerce Clause, even if he didn't have the courage of his radical convictions.

Still, to the judicial engagement crowd, Roberts's ruling has become Exhibit A in their case against judicial restraint. Roberts's opinion, Barnett has written, "illustrates how limited government has been undermined by creative doctrines employing the rhetoric of 'judicial restraint' to obviate the Constitution's text and facilitate unconstrained activism by legislatures." It's those democratically elected lawmakers, in other words, who are the real activists.

Now, with the next president likely to get the chance to appoint one or more new Supreme Court justices, Barnett and his allies are girding for the coming battle: achieving a Supreme Court with a majority that's willing to endorse judicial engagement and uphold the full range of economic rights that they believe the Constitution protects. In a 2015 *Weekly Standard* piece written with Blackman, Barnett noted the advanced ages of several of the current justices and explained what sort of candidate the next GOP president should choose to ensure a high court unafraid of striking down laws that violate the Constitution. The nominee, Barnett and Blackman wrote, should "reject clichéd calls for judicial restraint" of the kind that guided Roberts in the individual mandate case. "What really should matter to any constitutionally conservative voter or president," they explained, was this: "'Who has the fortitude to follow the Constitution wherever it may lead and let the chips fall where they may?'"

George Will has made clear what a Supreme Court like that would look like. "Ask this of potential court nominees," he wrote in a 2015 column, addressing the next GOP president. "Do you agree that *Lochner* correctly reflected the U.S. natural rights tradition and the Ninth and Fourteenth Amendments' affirmation of unenumerated rights?" In other words, do you want courts to unequivocally protect economic rights like the right of contract, potentially taking labor and other economic laws back to the nineteenth century?

There are signs that the Republican presidential candidates

are listening. It's true that most continue to blast the Supreme Court for doing too much on issues like same-sex marriage—"judicial tyranny," Ted Cruz has called it. And only one, Rand Paul, who quit the race after the Iowa caucuses, has come out as an explicit supporter of judicial engagement. "If we believe in judicial restraint, we presume the majority is correct," Paul said in a 2015 speech at the Heritage Foundation. "We presume that laws are constitutional until we can prove otherwise." Instead, he argued, "maybe we should start with the presumption of liberty." But the field may be further along the road to judicial engagement than they think. Several have denounced Roberts for his Obamacare vote—"I think he did it because he wanted to be popular in the Beltway," said Donald Trump. In doing so, they've implicitly endorsed Barnett's narrow reading of what kinds of regulation the Constitution allows. Especially if the next president is another Democrat, it's not hard to see a world in which judicial engagement becomes the consensus Republican position.

And after all, perhaps they've given up on the chief justice too soon. When it's gotten him to the result he's wanted, Roberts has been glad to practice an energetic form of judicial activism—and none more blatant than on cases with huge implications for the legitimacy of the democratic process itself. As we saw in chapter 1, in *Shelby County,* Roberts wrote the majority opinion striking down the central plank of the Voting Rights Act, which had been reauthorized almost unanimously by Congress seven years earlier. But he did so in the name of a dubious constitutional principle—the equal sovereignty of the states—that, as the scholars James Blacksher and Lani Guinier have noted, derived from the universally reviled *Dred Scott* decision of 1857, which held that blacks couldn't be considered full citizens. Here Roberts seemed to bend over backward not to defer to Congress but rather to find some constitutional pretext to rein it in.* In *Citizens United*, too, Roberts voted with the majority to strike down the McCain-Feingold campaign finance law's restrictions on independent political spending by corporations, based on a broad interpretation of the First Amendment. Each of these cases represented a double blow to democracy: first, because unelected judges relied on an expansive reading of the Constitution's prohibitions to strike down laws passed by democratic majorities; and second, because their real-world effects—relaxing barriers to racial discrimination in voting and making it much easier for the wealthy to drown out other voices in political campaigns—served to undermine the democratic process writ large.

And even in saving the individual mandate, Roberts approved, in theory at least, a more restrictive view of the Constitution than the Court has endorsed since before the New Deal. All that's needed next time is a little less respect for the democratic process. Barnett and his allies may be closer to victory than they think.

---

* Justice Scalia, meanwhile, went further. His reference during the oral arguments in *Shelby County* to the Voting Rights Act as a "racial entitlement" drew gasps. But that slur was in the service of a larger point about the shortcomings of democracy that was, if anything, even more astonishing. "Whenever a society adopts racial entitlements, it is very difficult to get out of them through the normal political processes," Scalia said. "I don't think there is anything to be gained by any senator to vote against continuation of this act." Scalia was arguing that the only reason Congress reauthorized by a lopsided vote the most successful civil rights law in history is that no one wanted to seem racist, and that as a result, racial issues shouldn't be left to the democratic process at all.

Chapter 6

PUSHING THE BOUNDARIES

In 2011 Rob Natelson wrote a paper for the *Tennessee Law Review* that, by the standards of the constitutional law world, went viral. A low-key and self-effacing Montana-based legal scholar with the conservative Independence Institute, Natelson likes to delve into obscure and poorly understood corners of the Constitution: areas like the Necessary and Proper Clause, or the Privileges and Immunities Clause, or the Indian Commerce Clause. Not exactly click-bait.

But this paper was different. It examined something called an Article V Convention—a way of amending the Constitution, never before achieved, by getting two-thirds of the state legislatures to call for a convention of state lawmakers. Beneath its academic prose and dispassionate tone, Natelson's article seemed to offer a way to sideline the federal government and restore power to the states. In the age of Obama, many on the right found that idea irresistible. "I just found a level of public interest that I had never encountered before with anything I'd ever written on," Natelson told me.

All of a sudden Natelson was overwhelmed with requests from political groups, academics, and legislators wanting to talk about Article V. ALEC asked him to produce a how-to guide to help states sign on. At an Article V "symposium" in Denver, he was feted like a visiting dignitary. Even Harvard Law School held an event on the scheme. Then in December 2013 more than one hundred lawmakers, the vast majority Republican, from thirty-two states gathered at Mount Vernon, George Washington's old Virginia estate, for an unusual meeting. After praying and reciting the pledge of allegiance, the legislators got down to the nuts and bolts of planning how to make an Article V Convention happen. Over the next twelve months, they held two more well-attended planning sessions, one at the Indiana State Capitol in Indianapolis, and one at the U.S. Naval Heritage Center in Washington, D.C., which was carried live on C-SPAN.

As of January 2016, twenty-seven states, most of them controlled entirely by Republicans, have passed resolutions calling for an Article V Convention to consider a constitutional amendment requiring a balanced budget. They've been helped along by ALEC, which has provided draft legislation. If seven more states sign on, Congress will, in theory, be required to call a convention for considering such an amendment. Four red states—Georgia, Florida, Alabama, and Alaska—want to go even further. They've passed resolutions calling for a broader Article V Convention that would let states propose amendments on whatever they liked, from making it easier to nullify federal laws to requiring photo ID to vote.

In other words, the campaign for Article V has moved well beyond the fringe. Aiming to woo conservatives ahead of the

2016 Iowa caucuses, Marco Rubio announced that on his first day in the White House, he would "put the prestige and power of the presidency" behind the idea, in order to pass a balanced budget amendment as well as term limits on Congress and the judiciary. Tom Coburn, the former Oklahoma senator and small-government zealot, has joined with a group created by Mark Meckler, a onetime national Tea Party leader, to promote Article V, which Meckler has called "a political inevitability" and "the 'sleeper issue' that will not only shape the 2016 presidential races, but will shape the course of our nation for decades to come." Randy Barnett, who's driving the judicial engagement movement, was pushing the idea just a few months into Obama's presidency.

To its most avid proponents, Article V is a way to use the Constitution to protect the Constitution, which they consider to be under threat both from the decades-long growth of the federal government and from the president's unapologetic use of his executive power on issues like immigration, gun control, and climate change. Indeed, the campaign has gained strength at a time when Constitution-worship is everywhere on the right. Tea Party senators write books about it. Activists offer courses in it. The GOP officially pledges a "restoration of Constitutional government" and calls itself the "party of the Constitution." Ted Cruz's campaign website contains a page touting his work to "restore the Constitution." And after Republicans won control of the House in 2010, they decreed that to kick off the new session, the document would be read aloud on the House floor. The exercise ran into trouble when some lawmakers balked at referring to slaves as three-fifths of a person—it was ultimately decided to skip the parts that had since been superseded by amendments—and again when a man interrupted by questioning President Obama's birthplace. But the point that Republicans really, really love the Constitution came through clearly enough.

As we'll see, this lionizing of the Constitution echoes a similar movement almost a century ago, which itself was a response to a series of major progressive accomplishments. Indeed, it's hard not to notice that for many on the right, our founding documents are primarily a device for short-circuiting democracy—and an alternative source of political authority that seems more likely to support the end goal of limited government. An Article V Convention is just one among several ideas that aim to seize on the Constitution to achieve outcomes that can't be won through the normal democratic process. Other conservatives have been toying with denying voters the right to elect senators, as the Constitution originally did, in the hope of getting a legislature that's more supportive of small-government principles. Campaigns are also afoot both to protect the Constitution's blatantly undemocratic system for electing the president and to rig it even further in the direction of the GOP. Perhaps most outlandish of all, one of the most prominent conservative scholars in the country has given up on the democratic process entirely, announcing that the only way to preserve the kind of economic rights that he believes the Constitution guarantees is to throw a wrench in the system.

Most of these strange, anachronistic-seeming campaigns stand little chance of coming to fruition, at least in the near term. But their surprising popularity sheds light on the level of the right's commitment to suppressing majority rule—for reasons both ideological and pragmatic—and the lengths to which conservatives in the Obama era are willing to go to achieve that end. Not content to stop at more conventional strategies, like voting restrictions and preemption, they're delving deep into constitutional minutiae in search of yet more creative ways to limit the power of the people and their elected representatives. Central to this project is a view of the Constitution as not just a guarantor of liberty but a check on democracy. "The United States is not in fact a democracy but a constitutional republic, and her virtues lie as much in her undemocratic institutions as in her ample provisions for self-rule—more, perhaps," one conservative writer reiterated recently in *National Review,* making the case for stripping voters of their right to elect senators. "It is liberty, not democracy, that is America's highest ideal."

Of course, proponents of Article V tend to say there's nothing antidemocratic about the scheme. Even with the big differences in the size of state populations, the amendment process is sufficiently difficult, they note, that it would be extremely unlikely that an amendment could get ratified—whether via Article V or the conventional manner—without the support of the majority of Americans.

But consider some of the ideas for amendments that have generated the most interest on the right: a balanced budget amendment; a stricter definition of the Commerce Clause; and what proponents call the Repeal Amendment, which would let three-quarters of states essentially nullify any federal law they didn't like, and which in 2011 won the support of the Republican House leadership. Versions of all three are included on a list that was drawn up and promoted by Mark Levin in a bestselling book, as well as in Governor Greg Abbott's "Texas Plan," which aims to "return lawmaking to the process enshrined in the Constitution." All aim to constrain the power of the elected president and of Congress to carry out steps they believe to be in the public interest. And there's one other amendment on the right's wish list that illustrates this reality more starkly than any other.

BY PRESIDENT GEORGE W. BUSH'S second term, Howard Stephenson had become frustrated that despite the administration's small-government rhetoric, federal spending continued to grow. A rigidly conservative Republican state senator from Utah, Stephenson was a kind of Tea Partier before his time. In a since-deleted blog post, he blamed the problem on his state's two Republican senators, Orrin Hatch and Robert Bennett, who he saw as having sold out their principles in favor of special interests. When Stephenson asked Hatch and Bennett why they weren't doing more to limit spending, he wrote, both told him flatly that they didn't answer to him.

This was the problem, Stephenson came to believe. As long as Hatch and Bennett were elected by the voters, it was too easy for them to use what he has called "mass demagoguery and vaguely tuned PR campaigns" to avoid accountability. That would be much harder if they were answerable to state legislators, a smaller, more sophisticated group. So in 2006 Stephenson introduced legislation to partially repeal the Seventeenth Amendment, which since 1913 has given voters the right to elect their senators directly. Until then, under the Constitution, that task had been entrusted to state lawmakers. Changing that status quo, Stephenson said, had been "a huge mistake."

That particular bill didn't go anywhere. But by 2010 much

of the rest of the GOP had caught up to Howard Stephenson. The Tea Party's rise that year was as much about political authority as about policy. At its core was the desire not just to shrink spending but to rein in lawmakers—especially Republican ones—who were seen as insufficiently committed to the cause of limited government. In that atmosphere, giving states more direct oversight of their senators, as the Founders had originally intended, was an idea with enormous appeal. All of a sudden, during that campaign, the need to repeal the Seventeenth Amendment was everywhere among conservative Republicans. Tea Party groups gave congressional candidates questionnaires that asked if they'd support repeal. It became a key point of dispute at Idaho's Republican convention. In Congress, Representative Louie Gohmert introduced a repeal bill intended, he said, as a way to stop Obamacare. Rick Perry came out against the Seventeenth Amendment, as did Justice Scalia, who blamed it for "the decline of so-called states' rights throughout the rest of the 20th century." Perhaps most sweetly for Stephenson, Mike Lee, an outspoken repeal supporter and "constitutional conservative," ousted Bennett in the Republican nominating contest in Utah and was elected to the Senate that fall. After Obama's 2012 reelection, which also saw Democrats pick up Senate seats, the idea gained some crucial new adherents—including Ted Cruz. "If you have the ability to hire and fire me, I'm a lot less likely to break into your house and steal your television," the Texas senator told an ALEC conference, where the group was mulling formally backing the idea. (It ultimately decided that repeal was "not germane to ALEC's mission of free markets, limited government and federalism.")

How did a significant faction of one of our major political

parties come to embrace so blatant an effort to roll back democracy? It helps to first understand how the Senate has been thought of both by the Founders who created it and by those who came after. As we saw in chapter 4, the decision that all states should have equal representation was mostly the result of a power play by the small states. But ideology also played a key role in shaping how the chamber would work. Most of the Founders agreed on a few broad principles, chief among them that the Senate should act as a check on the democratic passions embodied by the House, providing, as Madison put it, "more coolness" and "more wisdom."

But there was much less agreement on one key nuts-and-bolts question: How would senators be elected? Edmund Randolph of Virginia suggested that in order to check the "turbulence and follies of democracy," they should be chosen by members of the House. Delaware's George Read proposed a system where the president picked candidates nominated by state legislatures. James Wilson of Pennsylvania, among the more outspoken democrats at the proceedings, asked why not just have senators elected by the people, as in the House? But none of these ideas gained much traction. Eventually, it was agreed that senators should be appointed by state legislatures. The debate on the issue made clear that this was in order to protect not only the power of the states but also the interests of the wealthy. "Commercial & monied interest [will] be more secure in the hands of the state legislatures than of the people at large," predicted Elbridge Gerry of Massachusetts, because state lawmakers "have more sense of character, and will be restrained by that from injustice." Madison agreed that the "Senate should come from, and represent, the wealth of the nation."

But as the United States moved in a more democratic direction in the first half of the nineteenth century, this arrangement came to seem archaic. As early as 1826, there was a proposal in Congress for a constitutional amendment providing for the popular election of senators, but neither it nor a long series of similar measures over the next few decades succeeded. By the 1890s, though, there was a widespread belief that wealthy Senate candidates were buying the votes of state legislators, turning the chamber into a club for the rich. "It is as difficult for a poor man to enter the Senate of the United States as for a rich man to enter the kingdom of heaven," as one congressman artfully put it in 1898. That perception was strengthened when William Clark of Montana, an astronomically wealthy mining and banking entrepreneur, was forced to resign from the Senate in 1900 after an investigation found he had bought eight of his fifteen votes in the state legislature. (The Montana legislature promptly reelected him.) "He is a shame to the American nation, and no one has helped to send him to the Senate who did not know that his proper place was the penitentiary, with a ball and chain on his legs," wrote Mark Twain. Six years later an exposé in William Randolph Hearst's *Cosmopolitan* magazine by David Graham Phillips revealed similar vote-buying by Senator Nelson Aldrich of Rhode Island, a rubber and sugar magnate with a web of ties to corporate interests.

This outright corruption tied in to a broader charge leveled by the surging Progressive movement: that the Senate, despite its claims to wisdom and judgment, had failed to stop—indeed, had encouraged—the stunning Gilded Age consolidation of wealth in the hands of a small number of well-connected men. "What has the Senate done—the Senate, with its high-flown pretenses of reverence for the Constitution?" Phillips wrote. "It has so legislated and so refrained from legislating that more than half of all the wealth created by the American people belongs to less than one per cent of them." Requiring senators to face popular elections, it was increasingly felt, would make the Senate more responsive to the concerns of regular citizens.

Not everyone agreed. Some, like Senator George Hoar of Massachusetts, said explicitly that they didn't trust ordinary people to pick their representatives. "I think that it is best to commit this great function of choosing the members of this body to the deliberate and careful judgment of men who are trusted with every other legislative function of sovereignty, and not to adopt a method which in practice will commit it to men whom the people trust with nothing else," Hoar argued, perhaps forgetting that the people already elected their members of Congress as well as a host of state and local officers. Others made a related argument, one that underscored the reality that many conservatives continued to see the Senate in essentially antidemocratic terms. The whole purpose of the chamber, they contended, was to represent the states themselves, not the people. As one opponent of change put it, the states are "sovereign" and therefore are entitled to "a separate branch of Congress to which they could . . . send their ambassadors."

But these views were swimming against the tide. Led by lawmakers from western states, where progressive populism was especially strong, in 1912 Congress passed legislation that amended the Constitution to provide for direct election of senators. The following year, having been ratified by three-quarters of the states, the Seventeenth Amendment went into effect. For the first time in U.S. history—and within the lifetimes of at least a few Americans alive today—people could choose more than one in three of their national-level legislative representatives.

The Seventeenth Amendment was just one of a series of victories for the Progressive movement. Nineteen-thirteen also saw the Constitution amended to fulfill another Progressive goal: the creation of a federal income tax. It would be amended twice more over the next seven years to ban alcohol and to give women the vote. All this came on top of a raft of Progressive-backed measures passed by Congress—often prodded by President Wilson, today viewed by many on the far right, including Glenn Beck, as a historic villain—aimed at reining in the power of big corporations.

The result was a conservative backlash that, as now, combined a zealous fetishizing of the Constitution with frank expressions of fear about the consequences of popular rule. An influential 1913 essay by the Republican politician and diplomat David Jayne Hill—it was read into the *Congressional Record* by a supportive congressman—had set the stage, warning of a "crisis in Constitutionalism." The problem, Hill warned, was that demagogues were privileging "the will of the people" over the Constitution. By the early 1920s, conservatives had launched a campaign to revive (or perhaps create) an appropriate sense of reverence for the nation's founding document.

So many organizations sprouted to carry out this mission that an umbrella group, the Sentinels of the Republic, took charge, aiming to get one million Americans to "pledge themselves to guard the Constitution and wage war on socialism." They created sample laws requiring the Constitution to be taught in schools, which they submitted, ALEC-style, to state legislators. In 1921, by order of President Harding, the Constitution and the Declaration of Independence were moved from the State Department, where they'd long resided, to be displayed in the Library of Congress. There was a push to celebrate September 17 as Constitution Day, which in 1923 became Constitution Week. A 1925 contest in which high school students lectured on the Constitution was judged by the secretary of state and four Supreme Court justices, with President Calvin Coolidge in the audience. By 1931 forty-three states required constitutional instruction. At the same time, supportive historians recast the writing of the Constitution as the single key event of the founding period, saving America from the period of democratic turbulence after the Revolutionary War that had so discomfited John Adams. "There would be no Fourth of July celebration but for Sept 17 1787," wrote one, "because during the intervening years between the adoption of the Declaration of Independence and the signing of the Constitution, chaos and Bolshevism reigned supreme in this country."

This movement often presented itself as civics-based and ideologically neutral. But to many on the right, the Constitution seemed to offer a defense against all the problems of the age. "If the spirit of the Constitution prevailed, trouble between capital and labor would be minimized," the popular novelist Gertrude Atherton advised in 1922, "and were its meaning understood by immigrants, our immigrant problem would disappear." Indeed, as the historian Michael Kammen writes in *A Machine That Would Go of Itself: The Constitution in American Culture*, "an unconcealed criticism of democracy," pervaded this movement. Many conservatives saw democracy as a way station on the road to the socialism or outright anarchism that seemed to be threatening Europe in the wake of the First World War. In a 1924 essay that was published with a foreword by President Coolidge, U.S. solicitor general James Beck denounced "individualistic democracy," which he associated with Jefferson. Democracy, Beck continued, is "an institution which is tempered by wise and noble leadership, and in the case of America by constitutional limitations on the power of the masses." The Founders' "main purpose," Beck wrote approvingly, "was to defend their property rights from the excesses of democracy." Upon reading the essay, one admiring Chicago lawyer wrote to Beck, "I have come to the conclusion that democracy in government is a case of too many cooks (bad cooks) spoiling the broth."

It's perhaps no surprise, then, that a segment of the right—at times a fringe, at times less so—has never reconciled itself to the Seventeenth Amendment. During the 1950s and '60s, Robert Welch, the founder of the John Birch Society, kept the repeal torch burning among conservatives. In a 1966 essay Welch identified the democratic reforms of the progressive era as a key step toward communism. "For at least since the time of the Greeks it has been well known, as it clearly was to our Founding Fathers," wrote Welch, "that democracy was not only the worst of all forms of government, but was the last direct step of any nation and any people on the road to an unbridled mobocratic dictatorship."

Among the most troubling developments was the passage of the Seventeenth Amendment, Welch believed. "For as long as the senators for any state had been elected by the legislature of that state," he wrote, echoing the arguments of the amendment's opponents from half a century earlier, "they clearly represented the state itself as a sovereign entity within a federal union, and not just the citizens of the United States within certain boundaries, as was the case for the members of the House of Representatives." Cleon Skousen, a far-right disciple of Welch whose writing would later be popularized among Tea Partiers by Glenn Beck, picked up the theme, charging in a 1986 revisionist textbook that the "evil" Seventeenth Amendment had led to a "serious deterioration in states rights and state sovereignty."

But it was during the George W. Bush administration that the idea of letting state lawmakers once again pick senators began to once again move into the mainstream. In 2004 Zell Miller, an ultraconservative Democratic senator from Georgia who was then in the process of breaking with his party, introduced a bill to repeal the Seventeenth Amendment, framing it as a way to fight back against "extravagant spending" and "unfunded mandates" being put on the states. Alan Keyes, the Republican gadfly, picked up the idea a few months later as he ran for a U.S. Senate seat from Illinois. "Senators were originally chosen by the state legislatures for the simple reason that the U.S. Senate was supposed to represent the state government as sovereign entities," Keyes explained to his Democratic opponent, a state senator named Barack Obama, during a debate. Replied Obama, "I understand that's how the Constitution was framed. It also prohibited anyone but white, male property owners from voting. That's why we had amendments. It's a funny way to empower people to take their vote away."

Obama's riposte underscored the political dangers of trying to strip power from voters. Indeed, Republican congressional leaders always understood that the issue might appeal to some on the hard right but was a losing strategy with the broader electorate. Despite widespread promotion from the likes of Stephenson and Cruz, the GOP establishment managed to fight off the repeal campaign, and these days the idea has lost momentum even among the Tea Party crowd. But as the antidemocratic ideology behind repeal has moved back toward the mainstream, another brazen campaign has risen to take its place.

IF THE FOUNDERS didn't trust regular people to elect their senators, it's hardly a surprise that they didn't trust them to elect the occupant of the highest office in the land, either. That's why they created the two-step process of the Electoral College. State legislatures would choose presidential electors through whatever process they thought best, but it was well understood that they would be prominent local residents. Then these "most enlightened and respectable citizens," as John Jay put it in Federalist number 64, would use their superior judgment to select the president.

Thanks to the development of a party system in the 1790s, the Founders' antidemocratic vision for the Electoral College was never fully realized. Instead, electors soon began to run as members of a party slate, making clear that they would rubber-stamp their party's nominee rather than using their independent judgment. And almost all states soon turned over the task of choosing electors to voters rather than legislators.

Still, that's left us with a convoluted—and deeply problematic—system. Since almost all states award their Electoral College votes on a winner-take-all basis, you do just as well if you win a state by one vote as if you win it by one million. Then factor in that the allocation of electoral votes isn't even proportional to the states' sizes: every state gets at least three, creating a bias toward small states. It's not hard to see how this odd system has handed the presidency to the candidate who got fewer votes four times since the Founding, or in one out of fourteen elections. That's not to mention how the system encourages presidential candidates to focus intensely on swing states at the expense of the rest of the country. Or the unsettling reality that the electors are even today technically allowed to vote for whoever they want rather than for the candidate to whom they were pledged.

It's simply not possible to justify this system on democratic grounds. Sanford Levinson, the respected Harvard Law School constitutional scholar, calls it "indefensible." And so ever since 2000 a clever push to effectively end the Electoral College has been gaining steam among liberals and good-government types. The National Popular Vote (NPV) campaign lobbies states to pass legislation pledging that they'll award their electoral votes to the winner of the national popular vote—something everyone agrees is allowed under the Constitution. The legislation is written so as to go into effect only once states representing 270 electoral votes have signed on—at which point it would achieve its goal of ensuring that the candidate who gets more votes becomes president. To date, ten states plus the District of Columbia, representing a total of 165 electoral votes, have signed on to the plan. Aside from ensuring that the choice of the people becomes president, the NPV would end the distinction between swing and safe states, encouraging candidates to campaign across the whole country. "Here's a way that we can elect the president democratically," the *New Yorker* columnist and former Jimmy Carter aide Hendrik Hertzberg, a key backer of the idea, has said. "We don't have to change a word of the Constitution."

But among conservatives, an operation to protect the Electoral College has been building just as actively. It's a campaign that underscores perhaps better than any other issue how, for many conservatives, the Constitution's antidemocratic features are those most worth fighting for. And it highlights just how weak the right's commitment to democracy really is.

Some conservatives simply say there's no pressing need for change. "Our system for electing a president has worked pretty well," Brad Smith, the conservative former FEC commissioner, wrote in a 2008 paper condemning efforts to sideline the Electoral College. "There is no real case being made that it will work better if changed—only that it will look nicer if one subscribes to one particular vision of how democracies should work."

To most of us, of course, the idea that the candidate who gets the most votes should win—especially when it comes to picking the occupant of the highest office in the land—isn't just one particular vision of how democracy should work. It's pretty fundamental. But others on the right go further than Smith. They're committed to the idea that allowing the candidate who got fewer votes to win isn't just no big deal—it's crucial to America's well-being.

That's the view of Tara Ross, a Dallas-based onetime lawyer whose 2004 book, *Enlightened Democracy: The Case for the Electoral College,* was glowingly blurbed by Ken Starr and Ed Meese, the conservative legal activist who served as President Ronald Reagan's attorney general. The Heritage Foundation, too, has pushed the issue, via Hans von Spakovsky, a key proponent of tighter voting laws. Ross and her allies argue that the Electoral College helps ensure that candidates seek votes not just from the most populous areas but from across the country as a whole.

Without it, "we could see the end of presidential candidates who care about the needs and concerns of people in smaller states or outside of big cities," Ross explains in an earnest online video she made in 2015 to promote the cause. Ending the Electoral College, Ross says, would "undo America."

Of course, it doesn't seem to bother advocates of this view that today the Electoral College narrows campaign activity to ten or so swing states, leaving the other 80 percent of the country ignored. But leave that aside. Even if the Electoral College did encourage candidates to campaign over a broader area, why is that so important that it trumps basic democratic principles? Because, to put it bluntly, the ultimate purpose of the Electoral College is to thwart majority rule. "The Founders had no intention of creating a pure majority-rule democracy," Ross explains. "They knew from careful study of history [that] pure democracies do not work. They implode. In a pure democracy, bare majorities can easily tyrannize the rest of the country. The Founders wanted to avoid this at all costs."

This argument doesn't make sense either, of course: occasionally handing the presidency to the candidate who got fewer votes does nothing to guard against tyranny. Still, it's been enough to make sure Republican-led states line up behind the Electoral College and its guarantee of undemocratic presidential elections. Not a single state that has voted for a Republican presidential candidate since 1988 has signed on to the National Popular Vote plan.

Some Republicans aren't content with simply defending an undemocratic system. They're looking to skew the Electoral College further toward the GOP. Currently, every state except Maine and Nebraska awards all its Electoral College votes to the winner of the state's popular vote. But Republican state lawmakers in Michigan, Wisconsin, Florida, Pennsylvania, and Virginia—all states that went twice for Obama—have in recent years advanced legislation that aims to change that. One relatively typical version of the plan, proposed in Pennsylvania, would have given just two electoral votes to the winner of the state's popular vote, then awarded the rest according to the winner of each congressional district—taking advantage of the House gerrymander to boost Republican presidential candidates, too. If that had been done in 2012, it would have given Mitt Romney thirteen of the state's twenty electoral votes, even though Obama won 52 percent of the popular vote.

To some proponents of the idea, it's a way to boost the influence of rural voters and reduce that of urban ones—reflecting that age-old conservative fear of the city-dwelling masses. Charles Carrico, a Virginia state senator who sponsored a 2013 bill to assign electoral votes by congressional district in his state, has said that the experience of being outvoted in the last two presidential elections taught the people of his rural district that "their votes don't mean anything" compared to those in "metropolitan districts." Mike Green, a Michigan Republican senator, agrees. "Michigan, which awards by popular vote, will often be swayed by voters in the Detroit area, while others in the state may select a different candidate," Green said by way of explaining his 2015 proposal to divide the state's Electoral College votes. And it's not just a few loopy state lawmakers who are interested. RNC chair Reince Priebus said in 2013 that rigging the Electoral College is something states that vote Democratic in presidential elections but are currently controlled by Republicans "ought to be looking at."

The election of Democratic governors in Pennsylvania and Virginia has, for now, removed the threat in those states. And though conservative state legislators continue to introduce these bills, there are enough qualms among mainstream Republicans to render them unlikely to succeed. But what's perhaps most revealing about the plan is what it betrays about its proponents: a striking lack of confidence befitting a party that no longer believes itself capable of winning a majority. After all, dividing up electoral votes in a given state only helps Republicans if they lose the popular vote in that state. If they win it, the plan backfires. It wasn't long ago that Virginia was about as solid a red state as exists, and Republicans acted as if they had a fighting chance in Michigan, Wisconsin, and Pennsylvania, too. Now, it seems, they're just desperate to cut their losses.

BUT IF GIVING UP on Virginia suggests a certain pessimism about one's chances of winning a popular majority, giving up on democracy writ large surely represents another level of desperation. That's what Charles Murray now advocates. A scholar at the American Enterprise Institute, Murray is best known among liberals for his book *The Bell Curve* (1994), cowritten with Richard Herrnstein, which posited that genetic factors as well as environmental ones explained racial differences in IQ scores. But Murray's *Losing Ground* (1984), which argued that social welfare programs tend to increase, rather than reduce, poverty, is among the most influential works of social science of the modern era. Not long ago, when Jeb Bush was asked what he likes to read, he named Murray. Rand Paul and Paul Ryan have sung Murray's praises, too.

In his latest book, *By the People: Rebuilding Liberty Without*

Permission, Murray explains the need for what he calls a "Madison Fund." Essentially a well-resourced law firm, the fund would defend Americans, typically business owners, who decide to simply ignore government regulations that they and Murray see as burdensome and unjustified. The idea is that if thousands of people insisted on drawing out their cases rather than simply paying fines and moving on, the government wouldn't have the resources to enforce the law. As simple as that, the regulatory state would be sabotaged. Murray has long been a staunch opponent of a robust social safety net. But now he's advocating civil disobedience—explicitly throwing his hands up about the chances of achieving his goals through the political process.

"The Madison Fund could get started if just one wealthy American cared enough to contribute, say, a few hundred million dollars," Murray writes, though he says it could be a "popular movement," too.

Curtailing federal power, Murray says, can't be done through conventional politics. Why not? Citing the work of the economist Mancur Olson, Murray writes that "advanced democracies inherently permit small interest groups to obtain government benefits for themselves that are extremely difficult for the rest of the polity to get rid of." It sounds technical and scholarly, but it's really little different from Mitt Romney's claim that 47 percent of the country "will vote for this president no matter what" because they've been bought off with government benefits. And it hearkens all the way back to the views of those nineteenth-century conservatives who argued that expanding the franchise would inevitably lead to an unfair redistribution of wealth.

"Let me offer the fundamental theorem of democratic politics," Murray goes on to write. "People who receive government benefits tend to vote for people who support those benefits."

Why exactly this is illegitimate, rather than simply the normal functioning of what most of us call democracy, is never spelled out in detail. But what's clear is that Murray is arguing not only that our particular democracy has gone off the rails but that all democracies will inevitably do so. The deck will always be stacked against those who want to shrink government, so it's not fair to make conservatives play by democratic rules. "A successful agenda for rolling back government through the normal political process would require Madisonian [Murray's term for supporters of limited government] majorities in both houses and a Madisonian president," Murray writes. "It's not going to happen. Nothing will change that situation. It is built into the way that advanced democracies function."

Murray's dismissal of democracy is so blasé that even Jonah Goldberg ("voting should be harder, not easier") protested during a public conversation with Murray soon after the book's release. "Isn't it . . . a sort of sign of surrender on democracy?" Goldberg asked, also calling the idea of civil disobedience "unconservative." ("My heart is with you. I'm trying to bring around my head," he assured Murray.)

"I think we have an extremely serious problem that does not lend itself to a solution by anything else," Murray replied, "except trying to take back some portion of the freedom, the God-given freedom, that has been taken from us."

We're unlikely to see a mass epidemic of civil disobedience challenging government regulations any time soon—though recent armed standoffs between right-wing extremists and federal marshals in Nevada and Oregon differ from Murray's plan only in their choice of tactics. Indeed, the whole panoply of envelope-pushing strategies that have gained support on the right during the Obama years suggests not only a profound loss of faith in conventional democracy but also a belief that desperate times call for desperate measures. As Murray puts it in his book's first sentence, "We are at the end of the American project as the founders intended it."

If you believed that—and if, like many on the right, you saw democracy more as a means to an end than as a good in itself—wouldn't you be willing to push the boundaries, too?

Chapter 7

JOINING THE BATTLE

In January 2015 Kelli Griffin walked into a federal courtroom in Des Moines, Iowa, to fight for her right to vote—as well as that of tens of thousands of other Iowans. She was the plaintiff in an ambitious lawsuit aimed at dramatically weakening the state's ban on voting by former felons. The suit was part of a broader push to challenge state laws that, five decades after the passage of the Voting Rights Act, still disenfranchise nearly six million Americans.

Griffin, a shy stay-at-home mom who never completed college, hadn't expected to find herself a crusader for democracy. But she also hadn't expected what happened to her when she went to vote in a local election in her hometown of Montrose in 2013.

Griffin had been through some hard times—a survivor of domestic abuse who had suffered from drug addiction, she was convicted in 2008 of a drug-related crime and served five years' probation. But now she was turning her life around, and voting was a rite of passage. She even took her four kids to the polls to teach them about the democratic process. "I felt good," Griffin told me during an interview in Des Moines hours after her court appearance. "I mean, it's one of the steps to being back into society, to fulfilling that I am just like everybody else. I mean, I've overcome a lot."

But not long after voting, Griffin got a worrying phone call from an agent with Iowa's Division of Criminal Investigation. He was parked outside her house, and he said he wanted to verify the signature on her voter registration form. A few months later Griffin was charged with perjury in connection with illegal voting. As what the state considers a habitual offender, she was looking at up to fifteen years in prison.

The charges stemmed from an aggressive two-year investigation into voter fraud led by Iowa's then–secretary of state Matt Schultz, a Republican who in 2012 had tried unsuccessfully to pass a voter ID law. Schultz, who went on to serve as the Iowa chair of Ted Cruz's presidential campaign, quickly blasted out a press release touting the charges against Griffin and eight others accused of voting illegally.

What had Griffin done wrong? When she began her probation for the drug offense in 2008, her lawyer told her that once she completed it, her voting rights would be restored. That was true at the time: in 2005 then-governor Tom Vilsack, a Democrat, issued an order automatically restoring voting rights to felons who completed their sentences, enfranchising around one hundred thousand Iowans. But in 2011 Governor Terry Branstad, a Republican, took over, and on his very first day in office, he reversed Vilsack's order. Rights restoration for felons would now be at the discretion of the governor, and candidates would need to complete a lengthy and confusing application process.

Five years later just eighty-two people have had their rights restored under the new regime.

At her trial, Griffin testified that she was unaware of Branstad's rule change, and a jury quickly acquitted her. "I was happy that I wasn't going to leave my children," said Griffin, "because I didn't know not only how I would handle that, but how my children would handle not having a mother."

Still, fighting the charges had cost Griffin about ten thousand dollars in legal fees. And something else didn't sit right with her: she still wasn't allowed to vote. That's what led to the lawsuit, brought by the American Civil Liberties Union. It aims to end once and for all the confusing system of partisan-driven changes to the law that led to Griffin's mistake, and it argues that the Iowa constitution's ban on felon voting should be read to apply only to crimes that threaten the integrity of the election process itself. It was heard by the Iowa Supreme Court in March 2016. If it succeeds, around twenty thousand Iowans who have completed their sentences will immediately have their right to vote restored, and tens of thousands more will benefit going forward.

Felon disenfranchisement laws—many of which were imposed after the Civil War by southern states looking for ways to suppress black political power—are being targeted in other states, too, though their Republican supporters aren't backing down without a fight. In April 2016, Virginia governor Terry McAuliffe issued an executive order that reenfranchised anyone who had completed his or her full sentence, affecting more than two hundred thousand people. Ten days later, state GOP leaders announced they planned to sue to block the move. Two months earlier, Maryland lawmakers had restored the right to vote to around forty thousand people after they left prison, overriding a veto by the state's Republican governor. And while Kentucky and Minnesota saw their voting rights measures stymied by Republican opposition, legislation is popping up in other states—including even Alabama, whose ban on voting by felons was instituted in 1901 to fight the "menace of Negro domination," as one state leader put it. There are even some grassroots efforts at reform in Florida, where a ban on voting by felons disenfranchises over 10 percent of voting-age citizens and nearly one in four African-Americans.

The nascent shift on felon voting has been driven in part by a broader reappraisal—including by many conservatives—of the harsh criminal justice and sentencing policies imposed from the 1970s through the 1990s, an approach now widely seen as a failure. "It's quite difficult from a policy perspective to say that someone who's been convicted of a crime for the rest of their life cannot come back and rejoin democratic society," Julie Ebenstein, a lawyer with the ACLU's voting rights program, told me. "The tides are starting to turn."

But it also is in sync with an emerging movement that's responding to the last decade's Republican-led attacks on voting by going on the offensive in order to expand access to the ballot, especially for marginalized groups. It's not just on voting, either. The right's war on campaign finance laws has triggered a powerful push to find ways of increasing small-dollar campaign contributions, so that the voices of very wealthy donors are balanced by those of regular people. There's even a growing effort to make gerrymandering harder. In sum, as the Obama era draws to a close, the determined conservative campaign to block the popular will finds itself countered by an equally urgent bid to make our political system more responsive to the wishes of ordinary Americans. Which side ultimately prevails will go a long way to determining whether we're able to build a fairer economy, curb global warming, and tackle the host of other pressing challenges that politics exists to address.

AS DESTRUCTIVE AS the last decade's wave of voter suppression laws has been, it's been met by a barrage of lawsuits from the Obama Justice Department and from civil and voting rights groups that have succeeded in limiting the impact of at least some of the worst restrictions. Over the last decade, voter ID laws in Pennsylvania, Missouri, and Arkansas have been struck down after challenges. In Ohio, some weekend voting was salvaged as part of a legal settlement brokered by the ACLU and others in response to the GOP's sweeping cuts to early voting. That means the Souls to the Polls drives that many black churches use to encourage their parishioners to vote will still take place this fall. Even the voter ID requirement in North Carolina's draconian, multipronged antivoting law was softened somewhat by lawmakers, whose hands were forced by a challenge by voting rights groups and the Justice Department. It will be thanks to the work of skilled and committed advocates at places like the ACLU, the NAACP Legal Defense Fund, the Brennan Center for Justice, the Advancement Project, and the Lawyers Committee for Civil Rights Under Law, as well as the Obama administration, that perhaps a million or more Americans will avoid disenfranchisement.

The Democratic Party is newly at the forefront of the fight, too. In recent years, largely in response to the Republican assaults on the franchise, Democrats have taken a clearer and more forceful stand in favor of making voting easier, giving the issue a higher profile than it has had since perhaps the civil rights era. That's mostly because they've have come to understand that a larger electorate is crucial to their chances of victory. As President Obama put it in 2015, "If everybody voted, then it would completely change the political map in this country."

It hasn't just been lip service. In 2014 the Democratic National Committee launched its Voter Expansion Project, aimed primarily at funding efforts to register and turn out more voters and to pass state laws that expand access to voting. In just the first four and a half months of 2015, 464 such bills were introduced or carried over from the previous session, according to a tally by the Brennan Center. That's as compared to 113 restrictive voting bills. Indeed, for all the attention that voter ID laws and other measures that limit voting have deservedly received, today there's as much energy or more for efforts to move in the opposite direction. "We've seen increasing momentum toward improving the voting system, and in particular voter registration, across the country over the last couple years," Wendy Weiser, the director of the Democracy Program at the Brennan Center, told me in December 2015.

Of course, one reason fewer bills restricting voting have been introduced in recent years is that so many have already passed. And until those laws are repealed, the left's push to expand the franchise will do little to ease these measures' effects on the mostly poor and nonwhite Americans targeted by them. Still, it's evidence that many blue states have at last joined the battle over voting and are looking for ways to encourage it. And at the forefront of this movement is an elegant idea that has the potential to bring millions of new voters into the fold.

Those who study voting say the voter registration process—

and in particular the deadline for registration, which is typically several weeks before an election—is one of the chief barriers to participation. It's especially burdensome for certain types of voters—primarily those who move a lot, who tend to be young, poor, and nonwhite. And so in 2015 Oregon passed a law— without a single Republican vote, naturally—to automatically register its citizens to vote when they obtain or renew a driver's license or state ID card. People who don't want to register must opt out, rather than those who do being required to opt in. By switching the default mode from "unregistered" to "registered," the state is expected to bring nearly half of its eight hundred thousand unregistered but eligible voters into the system, ex- panding the voter rolls by 10 to 15 percent. Several months later California passed a version of the Oregon legislation—again with no Republican votes—that is expected to bring a good chunk of its 6.6 million unregistered voters onto the rolls. Secretary of State Alex Padilla, a Democrat who sponsored the bill, called it "the largest voter registration drive in the nation's history." As of November 2015, legislators in eighteen states plus the Dis- trict of Columbia had introduced similar measures.[*] Support for automatic voter registration has quickly become a consensus position among Democrats. In a June 2015 speech in Houston, Hillary Clinton made the idea the centerpiece of a sweeping voting rights vision, saying it "would have a profound impact on our elections and our democracy." Two months later her top rival for the Democratic presidential nomination, Senator

---

[*] New Jersey's bill passed, but Governor Chris Christie, who was running for the Republican presidential nomination, vetoed it, saying it's already easy enough to register.

Bernie Sanders, introduced an automatic voter registration bill in the Senate, and since then the two have sparred over who's taken more leadership on the issue.

But the most ambitious voting proposals are coming from the local level, where some deep-blue cities are working to expand the franchise in far-reaching ways. The Twenty-sixth Amendment bars disenfranchising anyone eighteen or older on account of age but says nothing about those under eighteen—meaning there's nothing in the Constitution that prevents allowing teenagers to vote. Since 2013 Takoma Park and Hyattsville, both Maryland suburbs of Washington, D.C., have done just that, empowering sixteen- and seventeen-year-olds to take part in municipal elections. (In Takoma Park, they voted at twice the rate of everyone else.) San Francisco is exploring doing the same, and could put the issue on the ballot in 2016. There's even a proposal in Washington, D.C., to let sixteen- and seventeen-year-olds vote in presidential elections.

The idea is perhaps not as radical as it seems. Brazil, Austria, Argentina, and some states in Germany already have lowered the voting age to sixteen for some types of elections. Twelve U.S. states allow seventeen-year-olds to vote in primaries if they'll be eighteen by the November general election. And indeed, a growing body of scholarship suggests sixteen may be a better age than eighteen for teens to cast their first vote, since they're more likely to still be living at home, giving them a greater tie to their community. A 2012 study published in the *Brooklyn Law Review* highlighted psychological research that suggests "mid-adolescents" are perfectly capable of making mature judgments in unpressured situations like voting. It concluded that, based on "the democratic presumption of inclusion," states should lower the voting age.

New York City recently considered an idea that sounds even more controversial: letting legal noncitizens who have lived in the city for six months or more vote in municipal elections. In fact, there's plenty of precedent for letting at least some noncitizens vote. In 1848 Wisconsin, whose population was 35 percent foreign born, enfranchised anyone who had lived in the country for two years and had filed papers to become a U.S. citizen. Other sparsely populated midwestern states with large foreign-born populations soon took similar steps, with the goal of encouraging settlement. (It helped that most of the alien population were German farmers, who were seen, in the words of one Indiana politician, as "upright, honorable, and industrious.") Some states continued to let declarant aliens vote well into the twentieth century. Even today six Maryland towns already allow it.

Supporters of New York City's plan say plenty of noncitizens pay taxes and send their kids to public schools, so why shouldn't they have a say on what happens in their community? And, they add, politicians will pay attention to the legitimate needs of noncitizens only if they're voters. "Enfranchising noncitizens would make communities like mine more important to city-wide and state officials," the proposal's sponsor, Daniel Dromm, a councilman representing a multiethnic area of Queens, said in 2015.

Then there's the final frontier: mandatory voting. When President Obama mused about the idea recently, he triggered a round of feverish conservative nightmares about both totalitarian government coercion and hordes of disengaged and ill-informed Americans voting for redistribution. But plenty of advanced liberal democracies, including Australia, Belgium, and Brazil, mandate voting, and no one is hauled off to prison for noncompliance. (In Australia, the penalty is a fine of about twenty dollars.) As you'd expect, studies show that requiring people to vote reliably increases turnout.

Nicholas Stephanopoulos, a law professor at the University of Chicago, has outlined an ingenious and surprisingly credible plan to use local governments as the springboard for mandatory voting. It starts with a progressive city in a swing state—say, Cleveland or Denver—passing a mandatory voting law for its municipal elections. It would also need to hold those elections on the same day as federal elections—that is, the first November Tuesday in even-numbered years. That would have the effect of massively boosting turnout from the city's voters in those elections. In response, conservative counties might well pass their own mandatory voting laws, to avoid being swamped by urban voters in presidential and other major races. But it's harder for numerous smaller counties to act than it is for one big city. So before long, for the same partisan reasons, Republican-controlled state governments would mandate voting statewide. At that point, blue states would almost certainly follow suit. Before too long, you could have something close to compulsory nationwide voting.

That's a long way off, if it ever happens. But if nothing else, Stephanopoulos's scenario underscores how efforts to expand the franchise have often originated at the local level. As the election law scholar Josh Douglas has noted, some cities in Kansas and Ohio granted women the right to vote in certain elections in the nineteenth century. Property requirements, too, were first eliminated locally.

"The power of using local law to reform our democratic processes is that it can have a positive ripple effect throughout the country," Douglas, who teaches at the University of Kentucky, wrote recently. "Municipalities should enact local laws expanding the franchise, which will have a significant effect in the long run in both securing voting rights for more people and making our democracy stronger nationwide."

But it's in Texas where the battle between expansive and restrictive visions of democracy has played out perhaps the most starkly. The state's Hispanic population is growing rapidly, but in 2012 just 39 percent of eligible Hispanics voted. Democrats know that if that community ever voted at the rate of whites—61 percent in 2012—they could make the most important Republican stronghold in the country competitive.

And so in 2013, a group of Democratic operatives launched Battleground Texas, an audacious long-term bid to turn the Lone Star State blue. It will ultimately require turning out a good chunk of the nearly two million unregistered but eligible Texas Hispanics—all in the face of a lengthy and burdensome list of rules governing the voter registration process and the nation's strictest voter ID law. Indeed, though Battleground's organizers are looking to make Texas more hospitable ground for Democrats, the work they're doing is striking a blow for small-d democracy, too. Battleground's founder, Jeremy Bird, ran field operations for both of Obama's presidential campaigns, pioneering an organizing model based on an insight developed by Marshall Ganz, an influential theorist of progressive organizing who was Bird's professor at Harvard. Ganz wrote that potential voters are far more likely to respond to persuasion by their friends and neighbors than to campaign operatives or volunteers parachuting in at the last minute. That's why the Obama campaign spent over a year forging deep ties to voters in their communities—an approach that indisputably paid off on Election Day.

Battleground aims to apply those same techniques to Texas. "There are so many people who have never been asked to participate before," Jenn Brown, then the group's executive director and now the chair of its board, told me in 2014. "And now they are."

At a 2014 training session in McAllen, on the Mexican border, many of the young volunteers shared heartwrenching stories about what led them to get involved. One woman sobbed as she told the group how her mother, who lacks health insurance, was recently diagnosed with cancer. Another said she had been raped her first year in college and found no resources to help her. A young Iraq War veteran recounted how he had put college on hold and joined the military in part to help his family pay for the funeral of his father, who also had been uninsured. Battleground aims to register and mobilize the millions of Texans—overwhelmingly young and nonwhite and consistently ignored by the Republicans who run the state unchallenged—with stories like these.

With its white voters remaining solidly Republican and perhaps even getting more so, Texas may not be competitive for a decade or more. In 2014 Battleground Texas turned itself into the de facto field campaign for Wendy Davis, the Democratic candidate for governor, only to see her get blown out in November by Greg Abbott. Still, Battleground's leaders—backed by major Democratic funders and other heavyweight figures in the party—say they're in it for the long haul.

It's not just on issues of voting access that we've seen a prodemocracy backlash. In recent years, numerous states have sought to fight back against gerrymandering by taking redistricting out of the hands of partisan lawmakers and giving it to independent commissions. Today twenty-three states have some sort of commission—though in many, lawmakers still play a role—and several more are considering joining them. There's not enough evidence yet to make a definitive judgment, but some experts say states that use commissions appear to get fairer results and more competitive elections. These efforts got a boost from a surprising 2015 Supreme Court decision: Justice Anthony Kennedy sided with the Court's four liberals to reject a claim made by Arizona Republicans that such commissions violate the Constitution by cutting state legislatures out of the process. And President Obama unexpectedly threw his weight behind the cause in his final State of the Union address. Veering from his prepared remarks, he called for an end to "drawing our congressional districts so politicians can pick their voters, and not the other way around"—adding that he planned to travel the country to promote reforms that make it easier to participate in politics.

But it's on campaign finance where perhaps the most hopeful developments are under way. As the damage wrought by *Citizens United* and other recent decisions has come into focus, a campaign to pass a constitutional amendment overturning the ruling has gained steam. It's won backing from Clinton, Sanders, Nancy Pelosi, and a host of other leading Democrats. But changing the Constitution to wipe out *Citizens United* just isn't going to happen any time soon. Indeed, the smartest reforms are focused elsewhere: on finding creative ways to empower small donors to balance out the voices of the wealthy.

New York City gives candidates who agree to spending

limits six dollars in matching funds for each of the first $175 that an NYC-based donor contributes—making a $175 donation worth $1,225 to participating candidates. In 2013 the system allowed Bill de Blasio, the candidate preferred by racial minorities and the working poor, to stay competitive against opponents who attracted far more big-dollar contributions and ultimately to win election as the city's mayor. The program is often cited as a model for cities and states across the country.

Seattle now empowers ordinary people even more directly. In 2015 voters approved a ballot measure to create a program that gives every voter four twenty-five-dollar vouchers to give to a participating campaign of their choice, turning literally any voter into a potential donor. (As in New York City, campaigns must agree to spending limits in order to be eligible.) Two Yale Law School professors, Bruce Ackerman and Ian Ayres, argue that adopting a voucher plan nationally could not only empower ordinary voters but also boost political engagement at a time when participation is dwindling. Doing so, they've written, "would provoke tens of millions of dinner-table conversations: Who should get our democracy dollars? Who is really concerned about America and its future?"

Beyond these concrete proposals, a transformative new approach to the issue may be starting to take shape. The election law scholar Rick Hasen writes in a new book that reform advocates should stop playing the Roberts Court's game by trying to fit every campaign finance law into the "anticorruption box; that is, arguing that each one is motivated by a desire to prevent corruption." Instead, they should stand forthrightly for a system that gives everyone a roughly equal say. Hasen's argument has quickly been embraced by reformers. "The principle of equality governs most of our political processes," Lee Drutman, an expert on lobbying, wrote in response. "So why should campaign finance be any different?" With a new member of the Supreme Court set to replace Justice Scalia sooner or later, the effort to restore equality to the center of the debate over money in politics might have come at just the right time.

Some of the pushback has been broader. After Republicans gained full control of North Carolina's government in 2012, thanks in large part to Art Pope's political spending, they engineered an across-the-board hard-right shift. In 2013 alone North Carolina said no to expanding Medicaid under Obamacare, approved a tax plan that redistributes wealth from poor to rich, cut education by half a billion dollars, and passed an antiabortion measure that drastically reduced the number of women's health clinics in the state. And to help entrench itself in power for as long as possible, it also imposed one of the most effective gerrymanders in the country, weakened campaign finance laws, and passed the nation's most restrictive voting law. In short, the GOP turned a state that once was known as a rare bastion of southern moderation into a massive testing ground for pure conservative ideology, and offered a glimpse of the kind of world that the nationwide assault on democracy seeks to create.

In doing so, it pushed people like Terry Johnson to get involved in politics for the first time. Johnson, who lives about a half hour north of Charlotte, had been laid off from her customer service job in 2012, and relied on the $320 a week she got in jobless benefits to support herself and her two kids as she searched for work. But in July 2013 the state cut off those benefits as part of the Republican government's push to reduce spending. That left Johnson without enough money to buy school supplies for her ten-year-old or to afford gas to get to job interviews. "My son gets locked out of a lot of things because I don't have a job," Johnson told me. "That's why I go every Monday and fight."

Since 2013 North Carolina's Moral Monday protests have generated national attention, bringing the crusading passion and righteousness of the 1960s-era civil rights movement to today's efforts to protect voting rights, education, abortion access, and a robust social safety net. "Don't make any mistake, America," William Barber II, the state's NAACP president and Moral Monday's charismatic chief organizer and most prominent spokesman, told a racially diverse, overflow crowd that August at a rally I attended in the college town of Asheville. "This is no momentary hyperventilation and liberal screaming match. This is a movement. And we intend to win."

It has helped knock down the approval ratings of the state's Republican legislature, and its governor, Pat McCrory, who faces a tough reelection battle in 2016. Perhaps more important, often folding the concerns of the Black Lives Matter movement into its call for equality and justice, it's spawned offshoots in states across the South and beyond. And after the short-lived excitement of the Occupy Wall Street protests, it's shown that a broad-based, multi-issue, multiracial, progressive movement can have staying power even with a Democrat in the White House.

SOMETHING ELSE IMPORTANT has happened. As these campaigns gain strength, fights over democracy have become another front in our familiar partisan war, with progressives and Democrats usually pushing for more of it, and conservatives and Republicans almost always wanting less. In just one recent example, allies of Hillary Clinton in February announced the launch of a $25 million political organization aimed at challenging restrictive voting laws and advocating for expansive ones, as well as boosting minority turnout—the latest sign that for Democrats, making voting easier isn't just a moral imperative, it's a requirement for political success.

For an issue to be defined along partisan lines sounds like a recipe for paralysis—but this, too, may actually be a good thing. Yes, it would be nice to think that core principles like the right to vote or the need to ensure that everyone has a roughly equal voice in politics are beyond debate. But the fact is that they're not—and rarely have they been in the past. Far from being a universally accepted American value, democracy in the United States has always been contested and contingent. Establishing a republic in which all men are created equal only kicked off the debate—it didn't end it. Even when democracy has advanced, it's done so in fits and starts and without ever truly winning over those who fear its radical ability to empower ordinary people at the cost of those on top.

Indeed, every time it's looked as if we were heading toward a consensus in favor of full democracy, that prediction has proven optimistic. From the outset, plenty of prominent Americans worked actively against greater social and political equality in favor of a far narrower view of the Revolution's meaning. Amending the Constitution to ban racial discrimination in voting only led, in both North and South, to more devious measures to limit the franchise—a cycle now repeating itself after the Voting Rights Act seemed for a time to have settled the question. Passing laws that reduced the corporate political influence of the Gilded Age, then giving those laws teeth sixty years later, spurred a shockingly successful countermovement aimed at amplifying the voices of the superwealthy. And in recent years, grassroots campaigns that have let ordinary Americans set the direction of their own communities have seen themselves brutally reined in by business interests and their allies in state government.

Powerful forces in American life—including, right now, one of our two major political parties—have for centuries subscribed to an ideology that has never fully accepted democracy as a good in itself. They aren't likely to come around any time soon, especially when doing so would threaten their interests. That means the only way to guarantee a future that's more democratic rather than less is not through persuasion or compromise but via the difficult, long-term work of politics itself. It's work that's unlikely ever to be complete. But now, at last, both sides have joined the battle.

Epilogue

I n January 2016, Michigan governor Rick Snyder offered a mea
culpa to rival any ever given by an American public official:
Snyder admitted in a major speech that his administration had
left the predominantly black and low-income residents of Flint
to drink and bathe in lead-contaminated water for seventeen
months, while wrongly assuring them it was safe. The poisoned
water had been linked to a spike in Legionnaire's Disease in the
Flint area, which sickened 87 people and killed 10. "No citizen
of this great state should endure this kind of catastrophe," Snyder acknowledged.

The Flint fiasco was both an environmental crisis and a
marker of how those without resources or influence too often
bear the brunt of government's failures. But it was something
else, too: a case study in what can happen when you get rid of
democracy.

Not long after Snyder and the GOP took control of the state
in 2011, they launched an attack on local control that made
those ALEC-backed state preemption laws look like child's

play. In one of their first acts, they passed a law that empowered state-appointed "emergency managers" to take over all aspects of any local government that was in financial distress, even including dismissing elected officials. For years, a right-wing, Koch-funded Michigan think tank with ties to ALEC had been advocating for the move as a way to weaken collective bargaining for public employees and advance other conservative fiscal goals. (Snyder would soon appoint one of the group's top staffers as emergency manager of Pontiac.) But many of those in the cities where emergency managers were being considered saw the law as a patronizing rebuke, implying that ordinary people were no longer trusted to run their own affairs. Nonetheless, over the next few years, Snyder placed several heavily minority cities, including Detroit, under emergency managers, essentially abolishing any semblance of representative local government in those places. In one city, Benton Harbor, the emergency manager banned elected officials from taking any official action other than calling a meeting to order, adjourning it, and approving the minutes.

The cities where emergency managers were appointed were generally in dire fiscal straits—but that didn't make residents happy to have their democratic rights taken away. In 2012 opponents collected more than two hundred thousand signatures in support of a ballot initiative to scrap the measure. At first, Republican state officials claimed the petitions circulated by canvassers should be thrown out because they had used the wrong font size (seriously). After a court rejected that gambit, the measure was put before Michigan voters, who decisively approved the law's repeal. But Snyder and GOP lawmakers were unfazed: in a lame-duck session of the legislature, they simply passed a new emergency manager law, this time making sure to add an amendment that prevented voters from overturning it.

Flint had four different emergency managers between 2013 and 2015, and exactly who made the fateful decision to switch the city's water supply to the Flint River—a move undertaken to save money—is under dispute. What's clear is that one of them, Darnell Earley, who was in charge at the time of the switch, failed to respond forcefully to complaints from Flint residents about the quality of the water. And, long after dangerous bacteria had been found in the water, leading the city to tell residents to start boiling it before drinking, Earley's replacement, Jerry Ambrose, rejected an offer to reconnect Flint to Detroit's water system.*

Of course, that was hardly a surprise. Earley and Ambrose answered not to the citizens of Flint but to the governor. "State officials, in fact, don't *want* appointed managers to be responsive to local constituents," Richard Schragger, a University of Virginia law professor and an expert on local government, has written. "That is the whole point of appointing a manager—to prevent him or her from responding too readily to the costly demands of city constituents. When a manager has been appointed to govern a city, the state is functionally declaring that the local political process has broken down and cannot be trusted."

The day after Snyder spoke, a less-noticed bid to subvert

---

* As Flint's water problems began to gain attention in January 2015, Snyder removed Earley—but immediately put him in charge of Detroit's public school system instead. Earley resigned from that post a year later, after having been accused of turning a blind eye to unsafe conditions in the city's schools.

democracy was playing out one thousand miles to the south in Jackson, Mississippi. A race for the state house the previous fall had ended, remarkably, in a tie: 4,589 votes for the Democratic incumbent, Blaine Eaton II, and 4,589 for his Republican challenger, Paul Tullos. If the seat went to Tullos, it would give the GOP—which already controlled the senate and governorship—a supermajority in the house. That would allow it to push an array of tax cut proposals that had been blocked by Democrats, who argued that the state with the nation's highest poverty rate had more pressing needs. But state law called for the tied candidates to draw straws—and Eaton won.

The Republicans didn't give up, though. When the house convened in January, they found the flimsiest pretext to throw out five of Eaton's votes: In an apparently novel interpretation of state law, they claimed that these voters were required to provide written notice that they had moved from one precinct to another within thirty days of the election, and had failed to do so—meaning they should be disenfranchised. On that basis, they ousted Eaton and seated Tullos in his place. A day later state officials were discussing a major new corporate tax cut.

The events in Flint and Mississippi—not to mention the standoff over replacing Justice Scalia on the Supreme Court that played out not long after—seemed to underline that for many Republicans, brute political power counts for more than an adherence to democratic values. And as the 2016 elections approach, the assault on democracy has only gained strength. In February, just days before a local minimum wage increase was set to go into effect in Birmingham, Alabama, state Republicans approved a minimum wage preemption law. One *New York Times* writer called it "state-mandated wage suppression by an all-white majority of lawmakers against a majority black city." The next month, after Charlotte, North Carolina, banned anti-trans discrimination, the GOP legislature called a special session to ram through a bill that prevented cities from passing their own antidiscrimination protections, nullifying the Charlotte law. And just in case any cities were thinking about it, they snuck in a ban on local minimum wage hikes, too. That same week, Arizona went even further, passing a kind of "super-preemption" bill. It withheld state money from any locality that enacted any measure stronger than state law—putting at risk any local-level law aimed at helping workers or protecting public health, the environment, or civil rights. Scott Walker and the Wisconsin GOP found yet another way to make voting harder, passing a law that will eliminate, or severely complicate, the community voter registration drives that disproportionately help the poor and minorities. And Utah's legislature even passed a resolution calling for the repeal of the Seventeenth Amendment, with one Republican lawmaker saying that letting voters elect their senators was one of the "most unfortunate mistakes that our country has made."

But there have also been signs of hope. Bernie Sanders likely won't end up as the Democratic presidential nominee, but the surprising strength of his insurgent bid, with campaign finance reform at its center, has made clear that the issue—once dismissed by political pros as dry and process-oriented—is galvanizing rich and poor Americans alike. Donald Trump's rise only bolsters the point: cleverly, he has incorporated anger over money in politics into his personality-driven theory of change, emphasizing his disdain for lobbyists and special interests and portraying himself, accurately or not, as unbuyable. In sum, Sanders's and

Trump's unlikely success suggests voters are looking not just for an "outsider," but for someone who will make government more responsive to the needs of ordinary Americans.

More hopeful still has been an emerging recognition among progressives that tactics like the assault on voting, the flood of political money, and the gerrymandering of Congress are no longer separate issues, but instead are part of—yes!—a coordinated attack on democracy. In one sign of the shift in thinking, hundreds of activists came together in April for a series of high-profile events, including a march from Philadelphia to Washington and a sit-in at the U.S. Capitol where hundreds were arrested. The protest, known as Democracy Spring, aimed to press Congress to pass legislation both to reduce the influence of money in politics and to protect voting rights. A report issued in January 2016 by a coalition of progressive and labor groups similarly identified a broad-based "attack on democracy."

With that new understanding fast taking hold, the continued expansion of democracy in America has reached a hinge point. Whether we're able to address almost every serious real-world challenge we face will depend, ultimately, on the direction in which that hinge swings.

Acknowledgments

This book wouldn't exist were it not for Sarah Burnes. From the outset, her enthusiasm, encouragement, and rock-solid belief in this project inspired me to push forward. Every writer should have such a smart, knowledgeable, and engaged advocate in their corner.

The book wouldn't be worth reading without the brilliant and unflagging work of Emma Berry. She understood right away what was compelling about this idea—often in ways that I didn't—as well as how to execute it. She's a careful and sophisticated reader with an extraordinary ability to hone in on the weak points in a piece of writing. Her input immeasurably improved the finished product, while respecting a writer's independence and autonomy—a rare and valuable quality in an editor. I'm fortunate to have had the benefit of her talent and commitment.

Thanks to everyone at Crown whose excellent work helped get this book out into the world. Molly Stern and Annsley Rosner championed this idea from the start. Liz Esman, Rachel

Rokicki, Sarah Pekdemir, and Kevin Callahan worked tirelessly to bring it to readers. Janet Biehl and Christine Tanigawa caught errors and vastly improved the flow of the writing.

Eric Nelson provided important early encouragement and advice and helped to shape the ideas that ultimately underpinned this book.

Richard Wolffe and Beth Fouhy at MSNBC indulged my obsessive reporting focus on voting rights out of which this book grew. And they were in all ways supportive of this project throughout. More broadly, my MSNBC colleagues are inspiring people to be around every day. A special thank-you to the late Geoff Cowley, whose unflagging decency and belief in the power of journalism to make a difference continue to offer a path to aspire to.

Nate, I'm sorry for all the times you came into my study wanting to play, only for me to tell you I had to work. Thank you for somehow understanding. Annie, thank you for fighting to be with us. I can't wait to spend more time with you both.

I owe by far my biggest debt of gratitude to my wife, Cassi Feldman. Writing a book in eight months with a full-time job is a challenge. Doing it with two kids under four is a joint project, pretty much by definition. It simply would not have been possible without your amazing support and generosity and your willingness to take on so much. I feel incredibly lucky to have you as a partner—and to now be able to give back to you what you've given to me.

Notes

Introduction: The Great Obama Freakout

I   **"European-style socialism":** Full video of Yoho's appearance provided to author by People for the American Way.

I   **"I can't remember which":** Brian Tashman, "As Candidate for Congress, Ted Yoho Suggested Limiting the Right to Vote to Property Owners," RightWingWatch.org, May 20, 2014.

2   **some waited as long as seven hours:** Juliet Lapidos, "Florida Voting: Like 'a Third-World Country,'" *New York Times*, November 5, 2012.

2   **an estimated 200,000 gave up:** Scott Powers and David Damron, "Analysis: 201,000 Didn't Vote in Florida Because of Long Lines," *Orlando Sentinel*, January 29, 2013.

2   **He now sits on:** Eric Bradner, "Boehner's Challengers: Gohmert, Yoho," CNN.com, January 5, 2015.

3   **viewed more than three million times:** John Ziegler, "How Obama Got Elected: Interviews with Obama Voters," video posted to YouTube, November 16, 2008.

3   **A 2012 Howard Stern segment:** "Howard Stern Interviews Obama Supporters in Harlem," video posted to YouTube, September 24, 2012.

4   **"The low-information voters are now":** "TIME: Obama Appealed to Low-Information Morons by Losing First Debate

to Romney" (transcript), *Rush Limbaugh Show*, December 20, 2012.

4   **"There are 47 percent of the people":** David Corn, "SECRET VIDEO: Romney Tells Millionaire Donors What He REALLY Thinks of Obama Voters," *Mother Jones*, September 17, 2012.

5   **"free stuff":** "Governor Mitt Romney Tonight at a Fundraiser About His Speech Today Before the NAACP," *Gretawire*, Fox News, July 11, 2012.

5   **"very generous":** Awr Hawkins, "Romney Conference Call: Obama Won by Giving Free Stuff, Amnesty," Breitbart.com, November 15, 2012.

5   **"Our message is one of hope":** Sean Sullivan, "Jeb Bush: Win Black Voters with Aspiration, Not 'Free Stuff,'" *Washington Post*, September 24, 2015.

5   **"JesusLand":** Original image posted on Yakyak.org, November 3, 2004.

6   **"soon wastes, exhausts":** John Adams, "Letter to John Taylor," (1814), in *The Works of John Adams, Second President of the United States*, ed. Charles Francis Adams (Boston: Little, Brown, 1851), p. 6:484.

6   **"demagogism":** Quoted in Alexander Keyssar, *The Right to Vote: The Contested History of Democracy in the United States* (New York: Basic Books, 2000), p. 227.

6   **"It is more important for any community":** "Why the South Must Prevail" (unsigned editorial), *National Review*, August 1957. See also Carl T. Bogus, *William F. Buckley Jr. and the Rise of American Conservatism* (New York: Bloomsbury Press, 2011).

7   **"can only exist":** Ronald Reagan, "A Moment of Truth: Our Rendezvous with Destiny," delivered at testimonial dinner for Rep. John M. Ashbrook, Granville, Ohio, June 8, 1965, published in *Vital Speeches of the Day* 31, no. 22 (September 1, 1965), p. 681.

7   **"The Framers founded a republic":** Julia Shaw, "Is America a Democracy or a Republic?," *Daily Signal*, November 1, 2011.

7   **A discredited Republican president:** M. Alex Johnson, "Bush Signs $700 Billion Financial Bailout Bill," MSNBC.com, October 3, 2008.

7   **"Is the allure of a charismatic demagogue"**: Mark R. Levin, "The Obama Temptation," *National Review*, October 25, 2008.

8   **"ears are open to the promptings"**: Francis Parkman, "The Failure of Universal Suffrage" (1878), quoted in Keyssar, *Right to Vote*, p. 122.

8   **"establishes the way to demagogism"**: Alexander Winchell, "The Experiment of Universal Suffrage" (1883), quoted in ibid., p. 123.

8   **establish FEMA concentration camps**: "Debunking Web Myths About FEMA Camps" (transcript), *Glenn Beck*, Fox News, April 6, 2009.

8   **global ban on guns**: Viveca Novak, "International Gun Ban Treaty?," FactCheck.org, December 5, 2009.

8   **"spread the wealth around"**: "Questions over Obama's Off-the-Cuff Remark" (transcript), *America's Election HQ*, Fox News, October 14, 2008.

9   **Both of Obama's presidential campaigns**: C. J. Ciaramella, "Echoing 2008, Obama Campaign's 'Project Vote' Also Brings Back 1993 Memories," *Daily Caller*, August 25, 2011.

9   **Consider that in 2012**: "United States: Elections: Presidential Elections," Roper Center for Public Opinion Research, Cornell University.

9   **Obama's success in turning out these voters**: Dan Balz, "How the Obama Campaign Won the Race for Voter Data," *Washington Post*, July 28, 2013.

9   **By opening hundreds of field offices**: John Avlon and Michael Keller, "Ground Game: Obama Campaign Opens Up a Big Lead in Field Offices," *Daily Beast*, October 19, 2012.

9   **A poll taken in August 2012**: *Washington Post*–ABC News poll, conducted August 22–25, 2012.

9   **"sharp increases in party loyalty"**: Alan Abramowitz and Steven Webster, "All Politics Is National: The Rise of Negative Partisanship and the Nationalization of U.S. House and Senate Elections in the 21st Century," presented at the annual meeting of the Midwest Political Science Association, Chicago, April 16–19, 2015.

10 **voters who consistently floated**: Corwin Smidt, "Polarization

and the Decline of the American Floating Voter," *American Journal of Political Science,* October 2015.

10   **Those nonwhite voters who accounted:** 1992 presidential election exit poll results at "United States: Elections: Presidential Elections," Roper Center for Public Opinion Research, Cornell University.

10   **Single women made up 23 percent:** Rebecca Traister, "The Single American Woman," *New York,* February 22, 2016.

10   **a built-in advantage:** Ruy Teixeira, John Halpin, and Rob Griffin, "The Path to 270 in 2016," Center for American Progress, December 17, 2015.

10   **government should redistribute wealth:** Frank Newport, "Americans Continue to Say U.S. Wealth Distribution Is Unfair," Gallup.com, May 4, 2015.

11   **"The country at large":** Peter Beinart, "Why America Is Moving Left," *Atlantic,* January–February 2016.

11   **"You've got to have real security":** Jenna Johnson, "Trump Alleges Widespread Voter Fraud: 'This Voting System Is Out of Control,'" *Washington Post,* January 5, 2016.

11   **"at least he's a leader":** Nick Gass, "Trump on Putin's Alleged Killing of Journalists: 'At Least He's a Leader,'" *Politico,* December 18, 2015.

11   **casual endorsement of violence:** Jeremy Diamond, "Trump on Protester: 'Maybe He Should Have Been Roughed Up,'" CNN.com, November 23, 2015.

11   **restricting freedom of the press:** Jose DelReal, "Trump, Taking Aim at the Press, Vows Again to 'Open Libel Laws,'" *Washington Post,* February 29, 2016.

11   **"The white American underclass":** Kevin Williamson, "Chaos in the Family, Chaos in the State: The White Working Class's Dysfunction," *National Review,* March 17, 2016.

12   **"Democracy is pretty popular":** Ari Melber, "RNC Rules: Insiders Speak Out on Contested Convention," NBCNews.com., March 18, 2016.

13   **a host of restrictions on voting:** "States with New Voting Restrictions Since the 2010 Election," Brennan Center for Justice, February 4, 2016.

14   **scrap meaningful limits on money in politics:** David Early and Avram Billig, "The Pro-Money Court: How the Roberts Supreme Court Dismantled Campaign Finance Law," Brennan Center for Justice, April 2, 2014.

14   **GOP-controlled states, with a major assist:** Ezra Klein, "House Democrats Got More Votes Than House Republicans. Yet Boehner Still Says He's Got a Mandate?," *Washington Post,* November 9, 2012.

14   **every trick in the rulebook:** Kevin Drum and Jaeah Lee, "3 Charts Explain Why Democrats Went Nuclear on the Filibuster," *Mother Jones,* November 22, 2013.

14   **crack down on the authority of cities:** Shaila Dewan, "States Are Blocking Local Regulations, Often at Industry's Behest," *New York Times,* February 23, 2015.

14   **a well-connected group of libertarian lawyers:** Ian Millhiser, "How Conservatives Abandoned Judicial Restraint, Took Over the Courts, and Radically Transformed America," *Think Progress,* November 19, 2013.

15   **"The real issue is that"**: Democratic debate in Charleston, S.C., January 17, 2016.

Chapter 1: Block the Vote

17   **The city of Beaumont, Texas:** Reporting trip to Beaumont conducted by author for MSNBC, September 2013.

17   **It was in nearby Jasper:** "3 Whites Indicted in Dragging Death of Black Man in Texas," CNN.com, July 6, 1998.

17   **"Fuck the niggers":** Joseph Lopez, "Man Arrested After Witnesses Say Gunman Shouted F*** the Ni**ers!" and Fired Shot at Crowded Campaign HQ," *12 News Now,* February 29, 2016.

17   **worked in the area as a young teacher:** Joyce Carol Oates, "Pilgrim's Progress," *New York Review of Books,* November 2, 2000.

17   **"did spend some time":** Joyce Carol Oates, tweet, March 12, 2013: "Have not yet journeyed to Hell nor even had a vision of it but did spend some time in Beaumont, Texas once."

17   **Like those of many American cities:** Alana Semuels, "Has

America Given Up on the Dream of Racial Integration?," *Atlantic*, June 19, 2015.

18   **its schools remained separate and unequal:** Patrick Michels, "Race to the Bottom," *Texas Observer*, November 14, 2014.

18   **"make 100 black men rich":** Ibid.

18   **In 2011 Getz and his allies:** Thomas Perez, assistant U.S. attorney general, to Melody Thomas Chappell, representing Beaumont Independent School District, December 21, 2012, U.S. Department of Justice.

18   **Indeed, at-large voting schemes:** "At-Large Voting: Frequently Asked Questions" (factsheet), NAACP Legal Defense and Education Fund.

18   **Thanks to overwhelming support:** Perez to Chappell, December 21, 2012.

19   **In March 2013:** Zachary Roth, "Breaking Black: The Right-Wing Plot to Split a School Board," MSNBC.com, October 17, 2013.

19   **the Justice Department intervened:** Thomas Perez, assistant U.S. attorney general, to Melody Thomas Chappell, representing Beaumont Independent School District, April 8, 2013, U.S. Department of Justice.

19   **In June 2013 the Supreme Court ruled:** *Shelby County, Alabama v. Holder*, 570 U.S. (2013).

19   **"racial entitlement":** Amy Davidson, "In Voting Rights, Scalia Sees a 'Racial Entitlement,'" *New Yorker*, February 28, 2013.

19   **"Our country has changed":** *Shelby County v. Holder* opinion.

20   **Just like that, the feds were:** Sarah Moore and Dan Wallach, "Ninth Court Reverses Ruling on November BISD Election," *Beaumont Enterprise*, October 17, 2013.

20   **Before elections under the at-large scheme:** Michels, "Race to the Bottom."

20   **But that was enough to convince:** Texas Education Agency, press release, April 14, 2014.

20   **"That would just cut":** Michael Getz, interview by author, Beaumont, Tex., September 5, 2013.

20   **"Things that we never thought":** Gwen Ambres, interview by author, Beaumont, Tex., September 6, 2013.

21   **Augusta, Georgia:** Sandy Hodson, "City Wins Lawsuit Over Change in Election Date for Local Offices," *Augusta Chronicle,* May 13, 2014.

21   **A host of southern states seized:** Tomas Lopez, "*Shelby County*: One Year Later," Brennan Center for Justice, June 24, 2014, http://www.brennancenter.org/analysis/shelby-county-one-year-later.

21   **In all, since 2006:** "States with New Voting Restrictions Since the 2010 Election," Brennan Center for Justice, February 4, 2016, http://www.brennancenter.org/new-voting-restrictions-2010 -election.

21   **All these laws disproportionately:** There is substantial evidence that all these restrictions on voting hit minorities, the poor, or the young hardest. For impact of voter ID laws, see "Issues Related to State Voter Identification Laws," U.S. Government Accountability Office, October 8, 2014. For racial impact of early voting cuts, see Bill Turque, "Early Voting Limits in Ohio Affect Black Voters Disproportionately, Study Says," *Washington Post,* October 8, 2012. For impact of voter registration restrictions, see Diana Kasdan, "State Restrictions on Voter Registration Drives," Brennan Center for Justice, 2012.

21   **people are more likely to be:** Tom Kertscher, "Which Happens More? People Struck by Lightning or People Committing Voter Fraud by Impersonation?" Politifact Wisconsin, April 7, 2016.

22   **Republicans understand that the lower the turnout:** Sean McElwee, "Why the Voting Gap Matters," Demos, October 23, 2014.

22   **"There is a deep-seated division":** Steven Mintz, interview by author for MSNBC, February 2014.

22   **Liberals, even at the Founding:** Universal Declaration of Human Rights, adopted by UN General Assembly, December 1948: "The will of the people shall be the basis of the authority of government; this will shall be expressed in periodic and genuine elections which shall be by universal and equal suffrage and shall be held by secret ballot or by equivalent free voting procedures" (Article 21).

23   **many conservatives have never:** Rick Hasen, "The New

Conservative Assault on Early Voting: More Republicans, Fewer Voters," *Slate,* February 10, 2014.

23   **That's how the eighteenth-century New Englanders:** Michael Schudson, "Voting Rites: Why We Need a New Concept of Citizenship," *American Prospect,* Fall 1994.

23   **"the stakes of politics are agreeably low":** George Will, "Federal Voting Drive Makes a Mountain Out of a Molehill," *Washington Post,* December 19, 2012.

24   **"Lower turnout sets the stage":** Will Wilkinson, "Thank You for Not Voting," *Ottawa Citizen,* October 22, 2008.

24   **"The need to register to vote":** Daniel Foster, "Don't Make Democracy More Like the Internet," *National Review,* June 4, 2015.

24   **"A small voting requirement":** Will, "Federal Voting Drive."

24   **"There was a time":** Steve Benen, "Building a Bridge to the 18th Century," *Washington Monthly,* October 5, 2011.

25   **"Is it time to revisit a test":** David Edwards, "Fox and Ann Coulter Prep for 2016: Bring Back 'Literacy Tests' So Voting Is 'A Little More Difficult,'" *Raw Story,* April 15, 2015.

25   **take the same test:** Jonah Goldberg, "Voter Apathy Isn't a Crime," *National Review,* June 27, 2012.

25   **"Voting should be harder":** Jonah Goldberg, "Voter Apathy Isn't a Crime," *Los Angeles Times,* June 26, 2012.

25   **raising the voting age to twenty-five:** Glenn Reynolds, "After Yale, Mizzou, Raise the Voting Age to 25," *USA Today,* November 16, 2015.

25   **"I've actually become more sympathetic":** Jason Brennan, *The Ethics of Voting* (Princeton, NJ: Princeton University Press, 2011), p. 76; Sal Gentile, "Are Bad Voters Like Drunk Drivers? New Book Says They Are, and That They Should Stay Home on Election Day," PBS.org, April 15, 2011.

26   **In the aftermath of the Revolutionary War:** Leonard L. Richards, *Shays's Rebellion: The American Revolution's Final Battle* (Philadelphia: University of Pennsylvania Press, 2003), pp. 4–19.

26   **"I . . . am much affected":** John Adams to Benjamin Highborn, January 27, 1787, in *The Works of John Adams, Second*

President of the United States, ed. Charles Francis Adams (Boston: Little, Brown, 1854), pp. 9:550–51.

26   **Starting in 1776, many states:** John Ferling, *Jefferson and Hamilton: The Rivalry That Forged a Nation* (New York: Bloomsbury Press, 2013) pp. 179–80.

26   **"spirit of independency was converted":** Quoted in ibid., p. 180.

27   **"The moment the idea is admitted":** Quoted in *The Political Writings of John Adams: Representative Selections,* ed. George A. Peek (New York: Hackett, 1954), p. xx.

27   **"Democracies have ever been spectacles":** James Madison, Federalist No. 10, *The Federalist Papers,* Yale Law School, avalon .law.yale.edu.

27   **Hamilton's famous advocacy:** Ferling, *Jefferson and Hamilton,* pp. 182–84.

27   **"rich and the well born":** Ibid., p. 186.

27   **"had pulled back the curtain":** Ibid., p. 187.

28   **"a trial of colors":** Quoted in Michael L. Mezey, *Representative Democracy: Legislators and their Constituents* (Lanham, MD: Rowman & Littlefield, 2008), p. 15.

28   **"should have as little to do":** Quoted in Mark David Hall, *Roger Sherman and the Creation of the American Republic* (New York: Oxford University Press, 2013), p. 95.

28   **"no end of it":** Quoted in Alexander Keyssar, *The Right to Vote: The Contested History of Democracy in the United States* (New York: Basic Books, 2000), p. 13.

29   **"darling privilege of free men":** Quoted in ibid., p. 9.

29   **In the end, it was agreed:** Ibid., p. 24.

29   **And so at the outset:** Ibid., table A2, p. 342.

29   **As part of a broader egalitarian trend:** Ibid., pp. 26–52.

29   **letting noncitizens vote:** Ibid., p. 33.

29   **Many of the Founders had believed:** Ferling, *Jefferson and Hamilton,* pp. 132–33.

29   **"is rapidly swelling":** Quoted in Arthur E. Sutherland, "Lawmaking by Popular Vote," *Cornell Law Quarterly,* December 1938.

29   **"Universal suffrage jeopardizes property":** Quoted in Keyssar, *Right to Vote,* pp. 48–49.

30   **In 1840 New York's Whigs:** Keyssar, *Right to Vote,* pp. 65, 66, 84.

31   **"while you shall not disfranchise":** The account of the debate over the Fifteenth Amendment is taken from ibid., pp. 93–104.

31   **In the South, Democrats used literacy tests:** Ibid., pp. 111–16.

31   **Northern Republicans used their own schemes:** Ibid., pp. 129–46.

31   **over 27 million immigrants:** U.S. Census Bureau, *Historical Statistics of the United States* (1976).

31   **"A New England village":** Quoted in Keyssar, *Right to Vote,* p. 122.

32   **"The opposition [to women's suffrage]":** Quoted in ibid., pp. 201–2.

32   **The Second World War and its aftermath:** Ibid., pp. 241–53.

32   **in 1961, after over half a decade:** "1961 U.S. Commission on Civil Rights Report Book 1: Voting," University of Maryland.

33   **"Many States disqualify paupers":** Ibid., p. 140.

33   **And in fact the poll taxes:** Keyssar, *Right to Vote,* p. 281.

34   **spurred a conservative countermovement:** Ari Berman, *Give Us the Ballot: The Modern Struggle for Voting Rights in America* (New York: Farrar, Straus & Giroux, 2015).

34   **"crisis of democracy":** Michel J. Crozier, Samuel P. Huntington, and Joji Watanuki, *The Crisis of Democracy: Report on the Governability of Democracies to the Trilateral Commission* (New York: New York University Press, 1975), pp. 114–15.

35   **acknowledged that this was unlikely:** Gay Seidman, "Mr. Huntington Goes to Pretoria," *Harvard Crimson,* November 5, 1987.

35   **Turnout for the 1988 presidential election:** Presidential Election Turnout Statistics, American Presidency Project, University of California at Santa Barbara.

35   **"Who wins under this bill?":** House of Representatives debate on National Voter Registration Act, February 4, 1993, C-SPAN.org.

36   **In Virginia, the number of registered voters:** Virginia Department of Elections.

36   **The following year Jim Gilmore:** R. H. Melton, "Va. High

Court Panel Bars Voter ID Plan," *Washington Post*, October 23, 1999.

36   **"If you've been here long enough":** Catherine Overton, interview by author for MSNBC, November 3, 2014.

36   **A draft of the 2014 Texas GOP platform:** Brian Tashman, "The Five Craziest Planks in Draft Texas GOP Platform: Ban Morning After Pill, Ending Direct Election of Senators, Defunding ACORN," RightWingWatch.org, June 5, 2014.

36   **"What do you think is really going on?":** Matthew Boyle, "Election Integrity Activists: Obamacare 'Biggest Voter Registration Fraud Scheme in History,'" Breitbart.com, October 30, 2013.

37   **"epidemic":** Greg Abbott, "Helping Stamp Out Voter Fraud in Texas," *Hill Country News*, March 10, 2006.

37   **The Lone Star State's soaring Hispanic:** John Judis, "Yes, Texas Could Turn Blue," *New Republic*, October 26, 2014.

37   **After two failed attempts:** *Veasey v. Perry*, 135 S. Ct. 9 (2014), opinion of U.S. District Court Judge Nelva Gonzales Ramos.

37   **Those who didn't have one:** The state later reduced the fee to two dollars but didn't publicize the change.

38   **Finding that it discriminated:** Charlie Savage and Manny Fernandez, "Court Blocks Texas Voter ID Law, Citing Racial Impact," *New York Times*, August 30, 2012.

38   **But within hours of the Supreme Court's ruling:** Todd J. Gillman, "Texas Voter ID Law 'Will Take Effect Immediately,' Says Attorney General Greg Abbott," *Dallas Morning News*, June 25, 2013.

38   **"The poor should not be denied":** *Veasey v. Perry*, Judge Gonzales Ramos opinion.

38   **But after Texas appealed:** Adam Liptak, "Supreme Court Allows Texas to Use Strict Voter ID Law in Coming Election," *New York Times*, October 18, 2014.

38   **Texas's only competitive congressional race:** Gilbert Garcia, "New Study Suggests Voter ID Altered District 23 Race," *San Antonio Express-News*, August 8, 2015.

38   **The law remains in force today:** "Required Identification for Voting in Person," Texas Secretary of State.

39   **It's impossible to say how many:** For a noncomprehensive list

of news reports of Texans who were unable to vote because they lacked ID, see Zachary Roth, "Texas Sees Surge of Disenfranchised Voters," MSNBC.com, November 3, 2014.

39   **The district court found:** *Veasey v. Perry,* Judge Gonzales Ramos opinion.

39   **"would certainly have carried the state":** Christopher Uggen and Jeff Manza, "Democratic Contraction?: Political Consequences of Felon Disenfranchisement in the United States," *American Sociological Review* 67, no. 6 (2002): 777–803.

39   **And they didn't even consider:** Berman, *Give Us the Ballot,* pp. 209–13.

40   **"The individual citizen has no federal":** *Bush v. Gore,* 531 U.S. 98 (2000).

40   **Soon Karl Rove and his allies:** David C. Iglesias, "Why I Was Fired," *New York Times,* March 21, 2007. On Rove's role, see also John Bresnahan and Josh Gerstein, "Rove Testimony Contradicts Wilson's," *Politico,* August 12, 2009.

40   **A mysterious Washington organization:** Rick Hasen, "The Fraudulent Fraud Squad," *Slate,* May 18, 2007.

40   **Soon a handful of intrepid:** Dan Eggen, "Official's Article on Voting Law Spurs Outcry," *Washington Post,* April 13, 2006.

40   **a deceptively edited undercover video:** Justin Rood, "McCain Acorn Fears Overblown," ABCNews.com, October 16, 2008.

40   **ACORN stole the election:** Tom Jensen, "ACORN," Public Policy Polling, November 19, 2009.

40   **Wisconsin, Kansas, South Carolina:** "States with New Voting Restrictions Since the 2010 Elections," Brennan Center for Justice.

41   **Kris Kobach:** Trip Gabriel, "Kris Kobach Pushed Kansas to the Right. Now Kansas Is Pushing Back," *New York Times,* October 16, 2014.

41   **disenfranchise as many as 24,000:** Peter Hancock, "Citizenship Law Hits Young Voters, Low-Income Neighborhoods Hardest," *Lawrence Journal-World,* October 30, 2014.

41   **Like Texas, Alabama waited:** Kim Chandler, "Alabama Photo Voter ID Law to Be Used in 2014, State Officials Say," *Birmingham News,* June 25, 2013.

41   **They waited a month before passing:** Michael C. Herron and

Daniel A. Smith, "Race, *Shelby County,* and the Voter Information and Verification Act in North Carolina," *Florida State University Law Review,* 2015.

41   **"Yes, voting is a right":** Representative Ruth Samuelson, North Carolina House of Representatives floor debate, quoted in Megan C. Raymond, "Rationalizing Voter Suppression: How North Carolina Justified the Nation's Strictest Voting Law" (2014), Scripps Senior Theses, paper 451.

41   **the North Carolina law disenfranchised:** Isela Gutierrez and Bob Hall, "Alarm Bells from Silenced Voters," Democracy North Carolina, June 15, 2015.

41   **Ohio wasn't directly affected:** "Jurisdictions Previously Covered by Section 5 at the Time of the *Shelby County* Decision," on the website of the U.S. Department of Justice.

42   **all-day lines:** DNC-sponsored survey referenced on the "Election Law @ Moritz" blog run by election law professor Dan Tokaji at the Moritz College of Law, Ohio State University.

42   **the state took action:** *NAACP v. Husted,* U.S. District Court, Southern District of Ohio, complaint filed May 1, 2014.

42   **"Early voting means stubborn voters":** J. Christian Adams, "ADAMS: Eight Reasons for Halting Early Voting," *Washington Times,* February 5, 2014.

42   **Republicans cut evening voting hours:** *NAACP v. Husted* complaint; Tanya Somanader, "Ohio House Passes 'Nation's Most Restrictive' Voter ID Law That Would Curb Rights of Almost 900,000 Ohioans," *Think Progress,* March 24, 2011.

42   **Some of those moves:** "Ohio Voters Gain Greater Access to Ballot in ACLU Settlement," ACLU, April 17, 2015.

42   **"I think voting is a privilege":** Glenn Wojciak, "Online Voter Registration Proposed in Ohio," *Brunswick Post,* May 22, 2015.

Chapter 2: The Platinum Age

43   **"Understand where I'm coming from":** *State of Arizona v. Walker,* Court of Appeals of Arizona, November 2, 1995, review denied April 23, 1996.

43   **And yes, he did:** "ARIZONA: Legislator Pleads Guilty in Bribe Case," *Los Angeles Times,* February 20, 1991.

44   That operation was just: John Pacenti, "Walker Found Guilty of Conspiracy in AzScam," Associated Press, November 5, 1992.

44   "I'm trying to position myself": *State of Arizona v. Walker.*

44   Nearly 10 percent: *Arizona Free Enterprise Club's Freedom Club PAC v. Bennett,* 564 U.S. (2011), brief of state respondents.

44   accused of improperly intervening: Dan Nowicki, "Keating Five Scandal Still Dogs McCain, 25 Years Later," *Arizona Republic,* April 6, 2014.

44   governor was indicted for perjury: "Arizona Governor Indicted by State on Campaign Loan," *New York Times,* January 9, 1988.

44   stringent restrictions on lobbying: *Arizona Free Enterprise Club v. Bennett.*

44   professional influence peddlers continued: Kris Mayes and Michael Murphy, "Invisible Legislature: Lobbyists Bearing Gifts Solidify Grip on Capitol," *Arizona Republic,* December 22, 1996.

44   "A seamless interplay between": *Arizona Free Enterprise Club v. Bennett.*

45   "matching funds": Adam Liptak, "Justices Strike Down Arizona Campaign Finance Law," *New York Times,* June 27, 2011.

45   By 2008 two-thirds: Michael Beckel, "Arizona Public Financing Law Faces Major Supreme Court Test," Center for Responsive Politics, March 28, 2011.

45   Connecticut, Florida, Maine, Minnesota: Liptak, "Justices Strike Down Finance Law."

45   challenged the law's matching funds provision: *Arizona Free Enterprise Club v. Bennett,* opinion.

45   Not surprisingly, the participation rate: "First Look: Small Donors, Big Money, and the 2014 Elections," Public Campaign, November 21, 2014.

46   preventing corruption is the only permissible: *Buckley v. Valeo,* 424 U.S. 1 (1976), opinion.

46   "'Leveling the playing field'": *Arizona Free Enterprise Club v. Bennett,* opinion.

47   an enabler of politically engaged billionaires: *Citizens United v. FEC,* no. 08-205, 558 U.S. 310 (2010).

47   **In 1971 Ralph Winter:** Howard R. Penniman and Ralph K. Winter Jr., *Campaign Finance: Two Views of the Political and Constitutional Implications* (Washington, D.C.: American Enterprise Institute, 1971).

47   **Republicans had outspent Democrats:** Nelson W. Polsby, Aaron Wildavsky, Steven E. Schier, and David A. Hopkins, *Presidential Elections: Strategies and Structures of American Politics* (Lanham, MD: Rowman & Littlefield, 2012), p. 65.

47   **Nixon had had to veto:** "Political Broadcast Spending Veto Upheld by Senate," *CQ Almanac*, 1970.

47   **"A limit on what a candidate":** Penniman and Winter, *Campaign Finance*.

48   **"We are often exhorted":** Penniman and Winter, *Campaign Finance*.

48   **campaigns relied largely on volunteer manpower:** Robert E. Mutch, *Buying the Vote: A History of Campaign Finance Reform* (New York: Oxford University Press, 2014), pp. 3–4.

49   **The 1896 presidential election:** Ibid., pp. 21–22. McKinley stayed home while Bryan conducted whistle-stop tour: "William McKinley: Campaigns and Elections," Miller Center, University of Virginia. In 2015 a new book appeared celebrating McKinley and Hanna's political vision in laying the groundwork for an era of Republican dominance that would last until FDR. It was written by Karl Rove, who himself would be a pioneer in soliciting political contributions from the superwealthy over a century later.

49   **"There are two things":** Michael Beschloss, "Money and Politics Go Hand-in-Hand," ABCNews.com, May 23, 2001, http://abcnews.go.com/Politics/story?id=121651.

49   **By then concern about the impact:** Mutch, *Buying the Vote*, p. 19.

50   **"to prevent the great moneyed corporations":** Ibid., p. 20.

50   **"a group of human beings":** Quotes from Burgess and Perkins in this paragraph are from ibid., pp. 193–95.

51   **concern about the corrupting influence:** Ibid., p. 38.

51   **"[Corporate] stockholders":** Ibid., p. 51.

51   **barred corporations from contributing:** Ibid., p. 1.

51   **"you've got to get":** Katharine Seelye, "Bush Picks Industry Insiders to Fill Environmental Posts," *New York Times,* May 21, 2001.

52   **Teapot Dome in Wyoming:** Ibid., p. 93.

52   **Still, they do appear to have helped:** Ibid., p. 95.

52   **"this important political office":** All quotes in this paragraph and the next are from ibid., pp. 195–97.

53   **"made their money in the private sector":** Bradley Smith to Rick Hasen's Election Law listserv, October 10, 2015, quoted with Smith's permission.

53   **"made their wealth in the traditional":** Bradley Smith to author, January 17, 2016.

53   **President Richard Nixon's 1972 reelection:** On the reforms of the 1970s, see Mutch, *Buying the Vote,* pp. 132–39.

54   **And that fall voters:** Ron Elving, "Congressman's Exit Closes Book on 'Watergate Babies,'" NPR, January 31, 2014.

54   **Just a year after the new rules passed:** Mutch, *Buying the Vote,* p. 143.

54   **"It would be strange indeed":** Ibid., p. 149.

55   **"Money is speech and speech is money":** Ibid., p. 148.

55   **In a complicated, multipart:** *Buckley v. Valeo,* opinion.

55   **"distinctly nonegalitarian vision":** Mutch, *Buying the Vote,* p. 150.

55   **Under the logic of *Buckley*:** Ibid., pp. 150, 158.

55   **By the end of the century:** Ibid., pp. 167–68.

55   **John McCain centered his 2000 bid:** Alison Mitchell, "THE POPULIST APPEAL; The Inside Outsiders Behind John Mc-Cain," *New York Times,* February 6, 2000.

56   **A New Hampshire grandmother:** Dennis Hevesi, "Doris Haddock Is Dead at 100; Walked for Campaign Finance Reform," *New York Times,* March 11, 2010.

56   **Finally, in 2002, Congress passed:** William M. Welch and Jim Drinkard, "Passage Ends Long Struggle for McCain, Feingold," *USA Today,* March 20, 2002.

56   **In September 1988 an independent:** "Willie Horton 1988 Attack Ad," posted to YouTube, November 3, 2008.

56   **Six weeks after it aired:** 1988 presidential election results,

American Presidency Project, University of California at Santa Barbara.

56   **The prime mover behind:** Sean Cockerham, "The Man Behind Willie Horton Ads Has New Target: Hillary Clinton," McClatchy Newspapers, July 12, 2007.

56   **David Bossie:** *CBS Evening News*, July 13, 1992, posted on YouTube, June 11, 2008.

57   **a group called Citizens United:** Jeffrey Toobin, "Money Unlimited," *New Yorker*, May 21, 2012.

57   **Kathleen Willey:** Stephanie Mencimer, "The Man Behind Citizens United Is Just Getting Started," *Mother Jones*, May–June 2011.

57   **Clinton sexually harassed her:** "Willey Talks to '60 Minutes,'" CBSNews.com, March 13, 1998.

57   **Citizens United wanted to run:** Toobin, "Money Unlimited."

58   **Jim Bopp:** Mencimer, "Man Behind Citizens United."

58   **In 2007, in** *FEC v. Wisconsin Right to Life*: Toobin, "Money Unlimited."

58   **Still, Bossie felt:** Ibid.

58   **A lower court had been unimpressed:** Mencimer, "Man Behind Citizens United."

58   **brought in Ted Olson:** Toobin, "Money Unlimited."

59   **But limiting the scope:** Ibid.

60   **"The Government has muffled the voices":** *Citizens United v. FEC*, opinion.

60   **"Five Justices were unhappy":** Ibid., dissent by John Paul Stevens.

61   **Based on the broad antiregulation:** Adam Liptak, "Courts Take on Campaign Finance Decision," *New York Times*, March 26, 2010.

61   **they would weaken the Arizona public financing law:** *Arizona Free Enterprise Club v. Bennett*, opinion.

61   **the Court scrapped limits:** *McCutcheon v. FEC*, 572 U.S. (2014), opinion.

61   **"quid pro quo" corruption:** Fred Wertheimer, "*Citizens United* and Its Disastrous Consequences: The Decision," *Huffington Post*, January 14, 2016.

62   **justices upheld a Michigan law:** *Austin v. Michigan Chamber of Commerce,* 494 U.S. 652 (1990), opinion.

62   **The Court's 2003 decision mostly upholding:** *McConnell v. FEC,* 540 U.S. 93 (2003), opinion.

62   **But in *Citizens United,* the justices:** *Citizens United v. FEC,* opinion.

62   **"Any regulation must instead":** *McCutcheon v. FEC,* opinion.

62   **In the 2014 cycle the 1 percent:** Peter Olsen-Phillips, Russ Choma, Sarah Bryner, and Doug Weber, "The Political One Percent of the One Percent: Megadonors Fuel Rising Cost of Elections in 2014," Sunlight Foundation, April 30, 2015.

63   **By June 2015, just 158 families:** Nicholas Confessore, Sarah Cohen, and Karen Yourish, "The Families Funding the 2016 Presidential Election," *New York Times,* October 10, 2015.

63   **"foreign policy experience":** Fredreka Schouten, "Experts: John Kasich Political Ads Chart New Territory," *USA Today,* October 7, 2015.

63   **a super PAC backing Jeb Bush:** Theodore Schleifer, "Bush Raises Over $100 Million to Help His Campaign," CNN.com, July 10, 2015.

63   **Ted Cruz's campaign may:** Jack Moore, "The Raw Footage of Ted Cruz's Super PAC Ads Is Awkward and Incredible," GQ.com, December 3, 2015.

64   **all but neutered by its GOP members:** Michelle Conlin and Emily Flitter, "U.S. Authorities Unlikely to Stop 2016 Election Fundraising Free-for-All," Reuters, June 4, 2015.

64   **banning a slew of shady:** Paul Blumenthal, "FEC Deadlocks on Whether Campaigns Can Coordinate with Their Own Super PACs," *Huffington Post,* November 10, 2015.

64   **"I don't believe that they":** All quotes from Ann Ravel in this section are from my interview with her, September 26, 2015.

64   **Jeb Bush's super PAC may have:** Matea Gold, "Jeb Bush's Super PAC Burning Through Money with Little to Show for It," *Washington Post,* December 9, 2015.

64   **In 2012 a super PAC created by Karl Rove's group:** Michael Isikoff, "Karl Rove's Election Debacle: Super PAC's Spending Was Nearly for Naught," NBCNews.com, November 8, 2012.

64   **Newt Gingrich's 2012 presidential bid:** Theodoric Meyer, "How Much Did Sheldon Adelson Really Spend on Campaign 2012?," *Pro Publica,* December 20, 2012.

65   **the carried interest loophole:** Lynn Forester de Rothschild, "A Costly and Unjust Perk for Financiers," *New York Times,* February 24, 2013; Morris Pearl, "What the Carried Interest Tax Loophole Reveals About Our Corrupt Political System," *Hill,* October 16, 2015.

65   **And have you ever wondered:** Kevin Drum, "Chart of the Day: Republican Tax Plans for the Middle Class," *Mother Jones,* November 11, 2015.

65   **a whopping 40 percent:** Elaine Maag, Roberton Williams, Jeff Rohaly, and Jim Nunns, "An Analysis of Marco Rubio's Tax Plan," Tax Policy Center, February 11, 2016.

65   **just 13 percent of respondents:** Andrew Dugan, "As Taxes Rise, Half in U.S. Say Middle-Income Pay Too Much," Gallup .com, April 14, 2014.

66   **His largesse on Gingrich's behalf:** Carla Marinucci, "GOP Presidential Hopefuls Line Up to Kiss the Ring in Vegas," *San Francisco Chronicle,* April 24, 2015.

66   **"occupied territories":** Kenneth P. Vogel, "Christie Apologizes for 'Occupied Territories,'" *Politico,* March 29, 2104; "The Time Chris Christie Stood Up to Sheldon Adelson," *New Republic,* March 31, 2014.

66   **minimum wage should be high enough:** Benjamin I. Page, Larry M. Bartels, and Jason Seawright, "Democracy and the Policy Preferences of Wealthy Americans," *Perspectives on Politics* 11, no. 1 (2013): 51–73.

67   **Eighty-four percent of respondents:** Nicholas Confessore and Megan Thee-Brennan, "Poll Shows Americans Favor an Overhaul of Campaign Financing," *New York Times,* June 2, 2015.

68   **And 78 percent of respondents:** Greg Stohr, "Bloomberg Poll: Americans Want Supreme Court to Turn Off Political Spending Spigot," *Bloomberg News,* September 28, 2015.

68   **"It's a good thing we have a Constitution":** Bill Maurer to Rick Hasen's Election Law listserv, September 28, 2015, quoted with Maurer's permission.

Chapter 3: What Happened in Denton

69   **Over the last decade, oil and gas companies:** Sharon Wilson and Cathy McMullen, "Cracks in the Frack Wall," *Fort Worth Weekly,* May 28, 2014.

69   **For a while most residents:** Unless otherwise indicated, quotes from Adam Briggle in this chapter are from my interview with him, July 1, 2015.

69   **across the street from Apogee Stadium:** Adam Briggle, *A Field Philosopher's Guide to Fracking: How One Texas Town Stood Up to Big Oil and Gas* (New York: W. W. Norton, 2015), map, p. xiii.

69   **the potential health and environmental effects:** For fracking's impact on air, see "Fracking Fumes Air Pollution from Hydraulic Fracturing Threatens Public Health and Communities," NRDC Issue Brief, December 2014. For its impact on water, see Neela Bannerjee, "Fracking Has Contaminated Drinking Water, EPA Now Concludes," *Inside Climate News,* June 5, 2015.

70   **The activists would be vastly outspent:** Peggy Heinkel-Wolfe, "Ban's Foes Far Outspend Proponents," *Denton Record-Chronicle,* October 27, 2014.

70   **in Vladimir Putin's pocket:** Barry Smitherman to Denton mayor and city council, July 10, 2014, Texas Railroad Commission.

70   **59 percent of voters:** Max B. Baker, "State Drops Lawsuit over Denton Fracking Ban," *Fort-Worth Star Telegram,* September 17, 2015.

70   **one man said he'd been hospitalized:** Briggle, *Field Philosopher's Guide,* p. 278.

71   **"The democratic process is alive":** Gregg Levine, "Texas Messes with Denton," AlJazeera America.com, November 11, 2014.

71   **At 9:08 the following morning:** Briggle, *Field Philosopher's Guide,* p. 284.

71   **Saying that the oil and gas industry:** Kate Galbraith, "Oil's Financial Ties to Texas Legislators," *New York Times,* April 11, 2013.

71   **Republican lawmakers were competing:** Briggle, *Field Philosopher's Guide,* pp. 283–84.

71   **"misinformation and sensationalism":** Christi Craddick, "We Must Work Together to Find a Solution," *Denton Record-Chronicle,* November 13, 2014.

72   **"Local control's great":** Jim Malewitz, "Dissecting Denton: How a Texas City Banned Fracking," *Texas Tribune,* December 15, 2014.

72   **"We don't need a patchwork approach":** Jim Malewitz, "Denton Fracking Ban Could Spur Wider Legal Clash," *Texas Tribune,* July 25, 2014.

72   **It was approved 122–18:** Max B. Baker, "Denton Fracking Bill Sails Through Texas Senate," *Fort-Worth Star-Telegram,* May 4, 2015.

72   **A white paper sent by:** Briggle interview.

72   **"a patchwork quilt of regulations":** "Governor Abbott Signs HB40 into Law," press release, office of Governor Greg Abbott, May 18, 2015.

72   **Faced with the prospect of a costly lawsuit:** Max B. Baker, "Denton City Council Repeals Fracking Ban," *Fort-Worth Star-Telegram,* June 16, 2015.

73   **"unemployed college kids":** Quoted in Lauren Kuby, "ALEC and ACCE Pay-to-Play Meeting: In the Belly of the Beast in Scottsdale," *PR Watch,* December 14, 2015. Pick's bio is at the National Center for Policy Analysis (NCPA).

73   **In recent years, Republican-led states:** "States Push Back Against Cities Seeking Business Regulations," Associated Press, May 17, 2015.

73   **With help from deep-pocketed business interests:** Mary Bottari, "The ALEC-Backed War on Local Democracy," *PR Watch,* March 31, 2015.

74   **"I think it is the time of greatest risk":** Mark Pertschuk, interview by author, July 7, 2015.

74   **Texas has actually been something:** Ibid.; Eric Gorovitz, James Mosher, and Mark Pertschuk, "Preemption or Prevention? Lessons from Efforts to Control Firearms, Alcohol, and Tobacco," *Journal of Public Health Policy* 19, no. 1 (1998): 36–50.

75   **"While we're not married":** Tina Walls quoted in Robin Hobart, "Pre-emption: Taking the Local out of Tobacco Control," American Medical Association, 2002.

75   **many of those twenty states:** Pertschuk interview; "Preemption Takes Center Stage in 2015," Grassroots Change, November 7, 2014.

75   **passing increasingly strict gun laws:** "Preemption Takes Center Stage in 2015," Grassroots Change, November 7, 2014.

75   **Alcohol interests, for instance:** Eric Gorovitz, James Mosher, and Mark Pertschuk, "Preemption or Prevention? Lessons from Efforts to Control Firearms, Alcohol, and Tobacco," *Journal of Public Health Policy* 19, no. 1 (1998): 46.

75   **banning cities from providing:** Chris Welch, "FCC Overrules State Laws to Help Cities Build Out Municipal Broadband," *Verge*, February 26, 2015.

75   **In 1973 a staffer in the Illinois statehouse:** Bill Bishop, *The Big Sort: Why the Clustering of Like-Minded America Is Tearing Us Apart* (Boston: Houghton Mifflin, 2008), pp. 223–24.

76   **At first, ALEC pushed:** Calvin Sloan, "Newly Uncovered Documents Expose ALEC's Anti-Gay Past," RightWingWatch.org, December 4, 2013.

76   **Today ALEC drafts cookie-cutter:** "What is ALEC?" Center for Media and Democracy.

76   **to a football team:** Representative Mark Pocan, "Inside the ALEC Dating Service," *Progressive*, September 14, 2011.

76   **Exxon, the American Petroleum Institute:** Lisa Graves, "A CMD Special Report on ALEC's Funding and Spending," *PR Watch*, July 13, 2011.

76   **turned their focus to the local level:** Alan Greenblatt, "From Campaign Finance to Pot, Progressives Look to Local Voters," *Governing*, October 2, 2015.

76   **"I don't want everybody to vote":** Josh Glasstetter, " 'I Don't Want Everybody to Vote'–the Roots of GOP Voter Suppression," *Right Wing Watch*, November 5, 2012.

77   **It banned local public health measures:** Bill Lueders, "Banning Local Rules Is National Strategy," Wisconsin Center for Investigative Journalism, May 28, 2013.

77   **It banned local regulation of ride-sharing services:** Mary

Spicuzza, "Scott Walker Signs into Law Uber, Lyft Oversight Bill," *Milwaukee Journal-Sentinel*, May 2, 2015.

77 **Mississippi—the state with the nation's:** "Preemption and Public Health Advocacy," National Policy and Legal Analysis Network to Prevent Childhood Obesity, Change Lab Solutions, September 2013.

77 **Oklahoma passed a fracking ban ban:** "Oklahoma Is Latest State to Prevent Local Fracking Bans," Associated Press, May 29, 2015.

77 **Colorado officials have sued:** Bruce Finley, "Colorado High Court Hears Cases on City Oil and Gas Fracking Bans," *Denver Post*, December 9, 2015.

77 **Arizona and Florida banned local laws:** "Pre-emption of Local Public Health Laws," factsheet prepared by Centers for Disease Control and Prevention (CDC) Office for State, Tribal, Local, and Territorial Support, Centers for Disease Control.

77 **After Salt Lake City made restaurants:** "Herbert Signs Bill Banning Phony Caller IDs, Drive-Thru Cyclists," Associated Press, March 26, 2015.

77 **"Texas is being California-ized":** Quoted in Valerie Richardson, "Them's Fighting Words: Abbott Says Texas Becoming Too Much Like California," *Washington Times*, January 8, 2015.

78 **more than twenty-five different:** List posted on the website of Local Control Texas, http://www.localcontroltexas.org /#!legislation/cee5.

78 **bans on banning plastic bags:** Tom Benning, "Bills That Would Sack Texas Bag Bans Left Hanging in Committees," *Dallas Morning-News*, May 7, 2015.

78 **a ban on cities requiring landlords:** "Texas Legislature Bans Local Ordinances Protecting Voucher Holders from Discrimination," press release, via National Low-Income Housing Coalition, June 1, 2015.

78 **Don Huffines, a freshman senator:** "Undermining Local Control in Texas" (editorial), *San Antonio Express-News*, March 2, 2015.

78 **"We didn't do enough":** Quoted in Tom Benning, "Texas Legislators Mostly Kept Hands Off Local Control," *Dallas Morning-News*, June 2, 2015.

78   **"people streaming over the border":** Quoted in Michael Warren, "The Next Governor of Texas?," *Weekly Standard,* April 14, 2014. Indeed, Californians have been leaving the state in record numbers over the last decade, with Texas as their top destination—though the Golden State's recent economic rebound may be slowing that trend.

79   **This drive to weaken local government:** On immigration, see Steve Nelson, "Obama Loses Again in States' Immigration Lawsuit," *U.S. News and World Report,* May 26, 2015. On Obamacare, see John Daniel Davidson, "A New Lawsuit from Texas Sues the Government over Obamacare," *National Review,* October 29, 2015.

79   **Perry even mused about secession:** Alexander Mooney, "Texas Governor Says Secession Possible," CNN.com, April 16, 2009.

80   **"an encroachment on private property":** Quoted in Marissa Barnett, "Gov. Abbott Signs into Law Restrictions on Cities' Ability to Regulate Oil and Gas," *Dallas Morning-News,* May 18, 2015.

80   **"I don't consider local control":** Quoted in Patrick Svitek, "Housing Bill Brings Local Control Debate into Focus," *Texas Tribune,* March 10, 2015.

80   **"Liberty always trumps":** Matt Rinaldi, "Liberty Trumps Local Control," TribTalk, a publication of *Texas Tribune,* March 12, 2015.

81   **"I would ask them":** Quotes from Ellen Bravo are from my interview with her, July 7, 2015.

81   **Like many struggling cities, Milwaukee:** Marc V. Levine, "Is Wisconsin Becoming a Low-Wage Economy," University of Wisconsin–Milwaukee, Center for Economic Development, October 2014.

81   **Many of them are in the fast-food industry:** Bravo interview.

81   **a voter initiative requiring paid sick days:** Milwaukee Paid Sick Leave Initiative (2008), Ballotpedia.org.

81   **The local chamber of commerce:** Georgia Pabst, "Court of Appeals Reinstates Milwaukee Sick Pay Law," *Milwaukee Journal-Sentinel,* March 24, 2011.

81 **a restaurant-industry-backed measure:** 2011 Wisconsin Act 16, Wisconsin legislature.

82 **"patchwork government mandates":** Quoted in Georgia Pabst, "Walker Signs Law Preempting Sick Day Ordinance," *Milwaukee Journal-Sentinel,* May 5, 2011.

82 **nearly two thousand industry lobbyists:** Pocan, "Inside the ALEC Dating Service."

82 **"Labor and Business Regulation Subcommittee":** Brendan Fischer and Mary Bottari, "Efforts to Deliver 'Kill Shot' to Paid Sick Leave Tied to ALEC," *PR Watch,* April 3, 2013.

83 **Since that New Orleans meeting:** "Paid Sick Days Preemption Bills 2015 (map), National Partnership for Women and Families, http://www.nationalpartnership.org/issues/work-family /preemption-map.html.

83 **with restaurant industry lobbyists:** Fischer and Bottari, "Efforts to Deliver 'Kill Shot' to Paid Sick Leave Tied to ALEC."

83 **"not an easy task, since granting":** Quoted in Brendan Fischer, "Paid Sick Day Campaigns Gain Traction as ALEC Allies Push Back," *PR Watch,* July 30, 2014.

83 **mock budget that McDonald's created:** Annie-Rose Strasser, "McDonald's Tells Workers to Budget by Getting a Second Job and Turning Off Their Heat," *Think Progress,* July 15, 2013.

83 **The ensuing press coverage, along with:** Tim Murphy, "New York City Fast Food Workers on How They Get By on $8 per Hour—and What a Bump to $15 Would Mean," *New York Magazine,* September 25, 2014.

84 **have raised their minimum wage laws:** Table 1, "City Minimum Wage Law: Recent Trends and Economic Evidence," factsheet prepared by the National Employment Law Project.

84 **"Perhaps the biggest threat":** Quoted in Steve Arnold, "Undercover at ACCE: ALEC Offshoot Spins City and County Officials on Dirty Energy, Local Control," *PR Watch,* February 23, 2015.

84 **At least twenty-one states:** "Preemption Takes Center Stage in 2015," Grassroots Change, November 7, 2014.

84 **Oklahoma's 2014 law came:** Ned Resnikoff, "Oklahoma Bans City Minimum Wage Hikes," MSNBC.com, April 16, 2014.

84   **Governor Mary Fallin:** "Governor Mary Fallin to Address Legislators from Across the United States," ALEC press release, April 26, 2013.

84   **"Death Star":** Zack Ford, "Extreme Bill Would Override All Local Employment Laws, Including LGBT Protections," *Think Progress,* May 13, 2015.

84   **"co-ordinated attack on democracy":** Rod Kackley, "No Minimum Wage Madness in Michigan," PJMedia.com, July 29, 2015.

85   **most people support raising the minimum wage:** Bruce Drake, "Polls Show Strong Support for Minimum Wage Hike," Pew Research Center, March 4, 2014.

85   **wage growth has slowed:** David Chance, "U.S. Seems Stuck with Slow Wage Growth Despite Strong Jobs Data," Reuters, January 9, 2015.

85   **an ever-larger share of profits:** William Lazonick, "Profits Without Prosperity," *Harvard Business Review,* September 2014.

85   **a wage boost was put directly before voters:** Rachel M. Cohen, "Minimum Wage Measures Pass Easily in Four Red States," *American Prospect,* November 5, 2014.

85   **"You measure democracy not only":** Gordon Lafer, interview by author, July 8, 2015.

86   **"We could never win at the local level":** Victor Crawford, "Cancer Converts Tobacco Lobbyist: Victor L. Crawford Goes on the Record," *Journal of the American Medical Association* 274, no. 3 (1995): 199–200.

86   **"Already most Americans feel":** Mary Bottari, interview by author, July 8, 2015.

87   **Walker and his fellow Wisconsin Republicans:** "Scott Walker's Record on Voter Suppression," One Wisconsin Now, http://onewisconsinnow.org/scottwalker/elections/.

87   **Wisconsin Republicans introduced:** Mary Spicuzza, "Republican Bill Seeks to Limit Local Photo ID Cards," *Milwaukee Journal-Sentinel,* January 1, 2016.

Chapter 4: Rigging the Playing Field

89   **On December 14, 2012, a gunman:** James Barron, "Children Were All Shot Multiple Times with a Semiautomatic, Officials Say," *New York Times*, December 15, 2012.

89   **In the preceding years:** "Deadliest U.S. Mass Shootings 1984–2015," *Los Angeles Times*, December 2, 2015.

89   **"this time is different":** Mike Lillis, "Obama on Gun Control: 'This Time Is Different,'" *Hill*, February 13, 2013.

89   **"They need to not just look us in the eyes":** "Newtown Families Voice Support for Gun Control" (transcript), *60 Minutes*, CBS News, April 7, 2013.

90   **a bill that called for expanding:** Molly Moorhead, "A Summary of the Manchin-Toomey Gun Proposal," *Politifact*, April 30, 2013.

90   **Polls showed that around 90 percent:** Scott Clement, "90 Percent of Americans Want Expanded Background Checks on Guns. Why Isn't This a Political Slam Dunk?," *Washington Post*, April 3, 2013.

90   **Then, unexpectedly, the bill:** Aaron Blake, "Manchin-Toomey Gun Amendment Fails," *Washington Post*, April 17, 2013.

90   **power of the National Rifle Association:** Michael Bloomberg, tweet, April 17, 2013.

90   **Others blamed the four:** Bill Daley, "Heidi Heitkamp Betrayed Me on Gun Control," *Washington Post*, April 19, 2013.

90   **"strategic blunders":** Ruby Cramer and Evan McMorris-Santoro, "How Joe Manchin Blew It," *Buzzfeed*, April 17, 2013.

90   **"stunning collapse":** Ed O'Keefe and Philip Rucker, "Gun-Control Overhaul Is Defeated in Senate," *Washington Post*, April 17, 2013.

90   **Largely overlooked in the postmortems:** Blake, "Manchin-Toomey Gun Amendment Fails."

90   **But because Republicans had made clear:** Jonathan Weisman, "Senate Blocks Drive for Gun Control," *New York Times*, April 17, 2013.

91   **But under Obama:** "Senate Action on Cloture Motions, Motions Field," U.S. Senate.

91   **"If you act like you're the minority":** Sam Stein, "Robert Draper Book: GOP's Anti-Obama Campaign Started Night of Inauguration," *Huffington Post,* April 25, 2012.

91   **a fundamental imbalance in the design:** Ezra Klein and Evan Soltas, "The Gun Bill Failed Because the Senate Is Wildly Undemocratic," *Washington Post,* April 18, 2013.

92   **In January 2009, 1.8 million people gathered:** Robert Draper, *Do Not Ask What Good We Do: Inside the U.S. House of Representatives* (New York: Free Press, 2012), pp. xv–xxii.

93   **"By sabotaging the reputation":** Mike Lofgren, "Goodbye to All That: Reflections of a GOP Operative Who Left the Cult," Truthout.org, September 3, 2011.

93   **Obama's stimulus bill:** Unemployment rate for January 2009 as cited by U.S. Bureau of Labor Statistics (BLS).

93   **In the House, not a single:** Jackie Calmes, "House Passes Stimulus Plan with No G.O.P. Votes," *New York Times,* January 28, 2009.

93   **in the Senate, just three:** "Senate Vote on Stimulus Package," Associated Press, February 11, 2009.

94   **Joining with the conservative Democrat:** David M. Herszenhorn and Carl Hulse, "Deal Reached in Congress on $789 Billion Stimulus Plan," *New York Times,* February 11, 2009.

94   **The result? A final package:** Ibid.

94   **Today there's a consensus:** Paul Krugman, "How Did We Know the Stimulus Was Too Small?," *New York Times,* July 28, 2010.

94   **Ordinary Americans likely paid:** BLS statistics.

94   **in 2010, with the economy:** Gary Langer, "Exit Polls: Economy, Voter Anger Drive Republican Victory," ABCNews.com, November 2, 2010.

94   **The economy would keep limping:** Josh Bivens, "At 2.5 Percent, U.S. GDP's Growth Rate Signals That a Robust Recovery Has Yet to Take Hold," Economic Policy Institute, April 26, 2013.

94   **They stood in the way:** Leigh Ann Caldwell, "Why Do Republicans Oppose Unemployment Benefits?," CNN.com, February 7, 2014.

94   one of the most effective policies at spurring growth: "The Economic Benefits of Extending Unemployment Insurance," White House Council of Economic Advisers and the U.S. Department of Labor, December 2013.

94   They actively created crises: Judd Legum, "21 Things Republicans Have Demanded in Exchange for Not Shutting Down the Government or Tanking the Global Economy," *Think Progress*, September 30, 2013.

94   a 2014 effort by Senate Democrats: Ramsey Cox, "GOP Blocks Minimum Wage Hike," *Hill*, April 30, 2014.

95   The 2011 debt ceiling fiasco: Jack Balkin, "The Not-So-Happy Anniversary of the Debt Ceiling Crisis," TheAtlantic.com, July 31, 2012.

95   In the end, Obama blinked: Dylan Matthews, "The Sequester: Absolutely Everything You Could Possibly Need to Know, in One FAQ," *Washington Post*, February 20, 2013.

95   "a failed attempt to stage": Balkin, "Not-So-Happy Anniversary."

95   "98 percent": Daniel Strauss, "Boehner: I Got '98 Percent' of What I Wanted in Debt Deal," *Hill*, August 2, 2011.

95   "sugar-coated satan sandwich": Quoted in Matt Schneider, "Democratic Rep. Cleaver: Debt Deal Is 'a Satan Sandwich' Antithetical to Religion," *Mediaite*, August 1, 2011.

96   In thirty-seven states: "State-by-State Redistricting Procedures," Ballotpedia.

96   A new round of redistricting: Nicholas Confessore, "A National Strategy Funds State Political Monopolies," *New York Times*, January 11, 2014.

96   But not until the RSLC's REDMAP: Confessore, "National Strategy Funds."

97   That spring Gillespie flew: Jane Mayer, "State for Sale," *New Yorker*, October 10, 2011.

98   the RSLC raised $30 million: Olga Pierce, Justin Elliott, and Theodoric Meyer, "How Dark Money Helped Republicans Hold the House and Hurt Voters," *Pro Publica*, December 21, 2012.

98   675 state legislative seats: Dan Balz, "The GOP Takeover in the States," *Washington Post*, November 23, 2010.

98   **21 state legislative chambers:** "2012 REDMAP Summary Report," RSLC memo, January 4, 2013.

98   **they now ran both chambers:** Confessore, "National Strategy Funds."

99   **key redistricting battlefields:** "State Legislative Election Results, 2010," Ballotpedia.

99   **In statehouses across the country:** Pierce, Elliott, and Meyer, "How Dark Money Helped Republicans."

99   **Democrats cluster in denser areas:** Nate Cohn, "Why Democrats Can't Win the House," *New York Times,* September 6, 2014.

99   **a 2004 Supreme Court ruling:** *Vieth v. Jubelirer,* 541 U.S. 267 (2004).

99   **Pennsylvania's seventh district:** Daniel McGlone, "Pennsylvania Congressional Redistricting: We Have a Plan," Azavea Atlas, December 14, 2011.

100   **"communities of interest":** Justin Levitt, "'Communities of Interest' in State Redistricting Law,'" presentation to National Conference of State Legislatures, April 25, 2008.

100   **"shoring up":** Quoted in Zachary Roth, "How Section 5 Blocked a GOP Power Grab," MSNBC.com, June 6, 2013.

100   **The old lines for District 23:** "MALDEF Triumphs in Texas Redistricting," press release, Mexican American Legal Defense and Education Fund.

100   **Canseco was ousted in 2012:** Reeve Hamilton and Becca Aaronson, "Congressional Roundup: Gallego Closely Defeats Canseco," *Texas Tribune,* November 7, 2012.

101   **In four large states:** Rob Richie of FairVote.org to author.

101   **the RSLC had spent $1 million:** "2012 REDMAP Summary Report," RSLC memo.

101   **other states, including Florida, Virginia:** Sam Wang, "The Great Gerrymander of 2012," *New York Times,* February 2, 2013.

101   **in Ohio, for instance, 55 percent:** Rich Exner, "Gerrymandering Has Tilted Political Control in Ohio; Supreme Court Ruling Opens Door for Change," *Cleveland Plain-Dealer,* June 29, 2015.

101   **Democratic House candidates won about 1.4 million:** Wang, "Great Gerrymander of 2012."

101   **"There is no question":** Quoted in Bill Lueders and Kate Golden, "Redistricting Credited for GOP Success in Wisconsin Congressional Races," Center for Public Integrity, November 20, 2012.

102   **"contorted and contrived":** Alice Ollstein, "Scalia's Death Throws North Carolina's Upcoming Election into Confusion," *Think Progress,* February 17, 2016.

102   **REDMAP says it plans:** Amber Phillips, "The 2020 Redistricting War Is (Already) On," *Washington Post,* July 16, 2015.

103   **they'd have to win ten million more votes:** Rob Richie, "Republicans Got Only 52 Percent of the Vote in House Races," *Nation,* November 7, 2014.

103   **This setup has worked against:** Charles Babington, "GOP's Serious Small-State Edge Boosts Its Senate Hopes," Associated Press, April 2, 2014.

104   **Madison argued vociferously against the idea:** Madison's notes on the Constitutional Convention debates, June 29, 1787, Yale Law School, avalon.law.yale.edu.

104   **Connecticut's Roger Sherman proposed:** "Roger Sherman and the Connecticut Compromise," State of Connecticut, Judicial Branch, Law Library Services.

104   **While other parts of the Constitution:** Rosenfeld, "What Democracy?" *Harper's,* May 2004.

104   **Virginia, then the largest state:** Klein and Soltas, "Gun Bill Failed Because."

104   **A majority of Americans now live:** Daniel Lazare, "Abolish the Senate," *Jacobin,* December 2, 2014.

105   **"we never saw any of the positive":** Adam Liptak, "Smaller States Find Outsize Clout Growing in Senate," *New York Times,* March 11, 2013.

105   **larger states tend to be much more urban:** Babington, "GOP's Serious Small-State Edge."

105   **Many of Obamacare's details were:** Nate Silver, "The Real Problem with the Senate's Small-State Bias," Fivethirtyeight .com, August 3, 2009.

105   **Nonwhites make up 44 percent:** Lazare, "Abolish the Senate."

106   **Perhaps that's one reason:** Jens Manuel Krogstad, "114th Congress Is Most Diverse Ever," Pew Research Center, January 12, 2015.

106   **37 percent of the U.S. population:** Hope Yen, "Census: White Majority in U.S. Gone by 2043," January 13, 2013.

106   **Washington, D.C., which is nearly 50 percent black:** Mike DeBonis, "D.C., Where Blacks Are No Longer a Majority, Has a New African American Affairs Director," *Washington Post,* February 4, 2015.

106   **continued opposition by congressional Republicans:** Andrew Mollenbeck, "D.C. Appeals to Republicans for Expanded Voting Rights," WTOP.com, January 5, 2015.

106   **It's now easier than ever:** Bill Bishop, *The Big Sort: Why the Clustering of Like-Minded America Is Tearing Us Apart* (New York: Mariner Books, 2009).

106   **urban areas are becoming ever more Democratic:** Josh Kron, "Red State, Blue City: How the Urban-Rural Divide Is Splitting America Apart," TheAtlantic.com, November 30, 2012.

106   **urban states tend to be more populous:** Babington, "GOP's Serious Small-State Edge."

106   **even though Republican senators:** Dylan Matthews, "The Senate's 46 Democrats Got 20 Million More Votes Than Its 54 Republicans," Vox.com, January 3, 2015.

106   **10 percent of major votes in the Senate:** Liptak, "Smaller States Find Outsize Clout."

106   **The Manchin-Toomey gun control vote:** Klein and Soltas, "Gun Bill Failed Because."

107   **The 54 senators who voted:** Babington, "GOP's Serious Small-State Edge."

107   **A separate gun control measure:** Ibid.

107   **As if small states weren't favored enough:** Liptak, "Smaller States Find Outsize Clout."

107   **"previous question motion":** Ezra Klein, "How the Filibuster Was Invented," *Washington Post,* March 8, 2010.

107   **"We say the Senate developed the filibuster":** Sarah A. Binder, *Politics or Principle? Filibustering in the U.S. Senate* (Washington, D.C.: Brookings Institution Press, 1996).

108 **"It was evident that consumption of time":** Martin B. Gold and Dimple Gupta, "The Constitutional Option to Change Senate Rules and Procedures," *Harvard Journal of Law and Public Policy* 28, no. 1 (2006): 206–72.

108 **"is the only legislative body":** Quoted in ibid.

109 **But fatefully, the new rules:** Ibid.

109 **Even during the turbulent 1960s:** "Senate Action on Cloture Motions, Motions Filed," U.S. Senate.

110 **In the six years from the start of 1963:** Ibid.

110 **A deal in late 2013 ended:** Domenico Montanaro, Mark Murray, and Carrie Dann, "Hypocrisy All Around in 'Nuclear Option' Debate," NBCNews.com, November 21, 2013.

110 **a bill that would have provided a public option:** Dylan Matthews, "17 Bills That Likely Would Have Passed the Senate If It Didn't Have the Filibuster," *Washington Post,* December 5, 2012.

111 **"the American people should have a voice":** Mark Landler and Peter Baker, "Battle Begins over Naming Next Justice," *New York Times,* February 13, 2016.

111 **"This Republican intransigence":** Jeffrey Toobin, "Looking Back," *New Yorker,* February 29, 2016 issue (appeared online February 21, 2016).

112 **loose coalitions of interests:** Matthew Yglesias, "The Case for Partisanship," *Atlantic,* April 2008.

112 **Today political scientists describe:** Kathryn Pearson, *Party Discipline in the U.S. House of Representatives* (Ann Arbor: University of Michigan Press, 2015).

112 **In July 2009 Senator Al Franken:** Kevin Drum, "About That Filibuster-Proof Majority," *Mother Jones,* September 22, 2010.

113 **It's no accident that this brief interlude:** Emily Smith, "Timeline of the Health Care Law," CNN.com, June 28, 2012.

113 **In fact, after Brown's victory:** "What Is 'Deem and Pass'?," *Week,* March 17, 2010.

113 **That unusual process led to flaws:** David G. Savage, "Could a Wording 'Glitch' Doom Obama's Health Care Law?," *Los Angeles Times,* August 25, 2014.

Chapter 5: The New Judicial Activism

115   **Washington's Mayflower Hotel:** Sarah Kershaw and Michael Powell, "Just a Hotel? For Some, It's an Adventure," *New York Times,* March 20, 2008.

115   **the Mayflower hosted the annual convention**: "2009 National Lawyers Convention," Federalist Society.

115   **membership list has included:** James Oliphant, "Giuliani Hitches Star to Conservative Legal Group," *Chicago Tribune,* September 6, 2007.

115   **Ken Starr:** Jason De Parle, "Debating the Subtle Sway of the Federalist Society," *New York Times,* August 1, 2005.

115   **According to one history of the group:** Michael Avery and Danielle McLaughlin, *The Federalist Society: How Conservatives Took the Law Back from Liberals* (Nashville, Tenn.: Vanderbilt University Press, 2013); Michael Avery to author, December 29, 2015.

116   **That year the roughly one thousand attendees:** "2009 National Lawyers Convention," Federalist Society.

116   **Senator Jeff Sessions:** Philip Rucker and Robert Costa, "Trump Questions Need for NATO, Outlines Non-interventionist Foreign Policy," *Washington Post,* March 21 2016.

116   **Steve Forbes:** Blaire Briody, "Buffett, Bah! Steve Forbes on the Folly of Taxing the Rich," *Fiscal Times,* September 19, 2011.

116   **"Hey, Randy, do you have any thoughts":** Josh Blackman, *Unprecedented: The Constitutional Challenge to Obamacare* (New York: PublicAffairs, 2013), pp. 41–43.

116   **Sarah Palin was screaming:** Angie Drobnic Holan, "Sarah Palin Falsely Claims Obama Runs a 'Death Panel,'" Politifact .com, August 10, 2009.

116   **Republican lawmakers were warning:** Jeff Mason, "Obama Again Tackles 'Myths' on Healthcare Reform," Reuters, August 24, 2009.

117   **Tea Party activists called it tyranny:** Ian Urbina, "Beyond Beltway, Health Debate Turns Hostile," *New York Times,* August 7, 2009.

117   **"profoundly unconstitutional":** David B. Rivkin Jr. and Lee A. Casey, "Constitutionality of Health Insurance Mandate

Questioned," *Washington Post*, August 22, 2009; Rivkin and Casey, "Mandatory Insurance Is Unconstitutional," *Wall Street Journal*, September 18, 2009.

117   **The argument struck at the heart:** Elise Gould, "What Happens If the Health Insurance Mandate Is Overturned?," Economic Policy Institute, June 27, 2012.

117   **Gaziano thought Rivkin and Casey:** Blackman, *Unprecedented*, p. 44.

117   **"Why the Personal Mandate":** Ibid., p. 47.

118   **"judicial activism":** "Cases of Judicial Activism," Heritage Foundation, http://www.heritage.org/initiatives/rule-of-law /judicial-activism.

118   **For nearly a century, most conservative judges:** Carson Holloway, "The Libertarian Constitution," *National Review*, March 9, 2015.

118   **But proponents of the new judicial activism:** Randy Barnett, "Judicial Engagement Through the Lens of *Lee Optical*," *George Mason Law Review* 19, no. 4 (2012): 845–60.

119   **"for much of the period":** Ian Millhiser, "If You Want to Understand What's Happened to the Supreme Court, You Need to Listen to Rand Paul," *Think Progress*, January 16, 2015.

119   **"growth and development of universal suffrage":** Tiedeman excerpt at the Portable Library of Liberty, a project of Liberty Fund.

119   **"assault upon capital":** Quoted in Ian Millhiser, *Injustices: The Supreme Court's History of Comforting the Comfortable and Afflicting the Afflicted* (New York: Nation Books, 2015), p. 60.

120   **"right of contract":** *Lochner v. New York*, 198 U.S. 45 (1905).

120   ***Lochner*, which is often taught:** Millhiser, *Injustices*, pp. 102–6; Millhiser, "If You Want to Understand."

120   **First, in 1935 the Supreme Court struck down:** *A.L.A. Schechter Poultry Corp. v. United States*, 295 U.S. 495 (1935).

120   **nixed the Agricultural Adjustment Act:** *United States v. Butler*, 297 U.S. 1 (1936).

120   **Even coal mining:** William Leuchtenburg, "When Franklin Roosevelt Clashed with the Supreme Court–and Lost," *Smithsonian Magazine*, May 2005.

121   **Only after Roosevelt controversially tried:** Leuchtenburg, "When Franklin Roosevelt Clashed."

121   **"the very essence of ordered liberty":** Lincoln Kaplan, "Ruth Bader Ginsburg and Footnote Four," *New Yorker,* September 13, 2013.

121   **"the Court's first—and maybe only—attempt":** David A. Strauss, "Is *Carolene Products* Obsolete?," *University of Illinois Law Review,* July 7, 2010.

122   **"we trust the democratic process":** Quoted in Adam Liptak, "How Activist Is the Supreme Court?," *New York Times,* October 12, 2013.

122   **"Many of our politicians have surrendered":** Quoted in Vanessa Williams, "Huckabee: What If the Supreme Court Picked the President?," *Washington Post,* May 24, 2015.

122   **"What we reject is judges":** Randy Barnett, " 'Judicial Engagement' Is Not the Same as 'Judicial Activism,' " *Washington Post,* January 28, 2014.

123   **It's not that most courts:** Clark Neily, interview by author, August 8, 2015.

123   **"Under current doctrine, the Supreme Court":** Quoted in Jay M. Feinman, *Unmaking the Law: The Conservative Campaign to Roll Back the Common Law* (Boston: Beacon Press, 2004), p. 134.

124   **In 2011 the IJ launched:** "IJ Launches Center for Judicial Engagement," Institute for Justice, February 2011.

124   **"The Constitution itself blocks":** Neily interview.

124   **"In practice, the claim that laws":** Randy Barnett, "Book Review: 'Terms of Engagement,' by Clark M. Neily III," *Wall Street Journal,* November 19, 2013.

125   **"a rhetorical call to arms":** Suzanna Sherry, "Why We Need More Judicial Activism," Vanderbilt Public Law Research Paper no.13-3; Sherry, "Liberty's Safety Net," *Green Bag,* Summer 2013.

125   **The paper caused such a splash:** "Micro-Symposium: Sherry's 'Judicial Activism,' " *Green Bag,* Summer 2013.

125   **"The sovereignty of the people":** Randy Barnett, "My Federalist Society Debate with Judge Wilkinson on Whether Judges Are Too Deferential to Legislatures," Volokh Conspiracy, November 21, 2013.

126 **"The younger people"**: Quoted in Brian Beutler, "The Rehabilitationists," *New Republic,* August 30, 2015.

126 **In January 2016 Arizona's Republican governor:** Jonathan H. Adler, "Institute for Justice Co-founder Named to Arizona Supreme Court," *Washington Post,* January 6, 2016.

126 **"judicial imperialism"**: Ed Whelan, "George Will's Embrace of Judicial Activism," *National Review,* January 23, 2014.

126 **"in practicing what conservatives"**: George Will, "Judicial Activism Isn't a Bad Thing," *Washington Post,* January 22, 2014.

127 **Senator Orrin Hatch had it read:** Blackman, *Unprecedented,* p. 49.

127 **Within months, numerous Republican:** Warren Richey, "Attorneys General in 14 States Sue to Block Healthcare Reform Law," *Christian Science Monitor,* March 23, 2010.

127 **Most legal observers gave:** Ilya Somin, "Legal Action and Political Action as a Two-Track Strategy for Opposing Obamacare," Volokh Conspiracy, March 22, 2010.

127 **After all, in *Gonzales v. Raich,* in 2005:** *Gonzales v. Raich,* 545 U.S. 1 (2005).

127 **Barnett had argued that case:** Randy E. Barnett, "Limiting Raich," *Lewis & Clark Law Review* 9, no. 4 (2005).

127 **But the plaintiffs got around:** "Virginia Attorney General to File Suit Against Federal Government over Passage of Health Care Bill," press release, March 22, 2010.

128 **In January 2011 Florida district court judge:** Kevin Sack, "Federal Judge Rules That Health Law Violates Constitution," *New York Times,* January 31, 2011.

128 **"extremely deep in its discussion"**: Alexander Bolton, "Lawmakers Press Supreme Court for Verdict on Healthcare Law," *Hill,* February 2, 2011.

128 **Later that year a federal appeals court affirmed:** Brent Kendall, "Health Overhaul Is Dealt Setback," *Wall Street Journal,* August 13, 2011.

128 **But months earlier a different appeals court:** Noam Levey and David Savage, "Appeals Court Declares Health Law Constitutional," *Los Angeles Times,* June 30, 2011.

128 **Chief Justice John Roberts:** Lyle Denniston, "Don't Call It a Mandate—It's a Tax," SCOTUSblog, June 28, 2012. On

Roberts's reported change of heart, see Jan Crawford, "Roberts Switched Views to Uphold Health Care Law," CBSNews.com, July 2, 2012.

128   **"illustrates how limited government"**: Barnett, "Book Review: 'Terms of Engagement,' by Clark M. Neily III."

129   **Now, with the next president**: Rebecca Shabad, "How Could the Next President Reshape the Supreme Court?," CBSNews .com, January 5, 2016.

129   **"reject clichéd calls for judicial restraint"**: Randy Barnett and Josh Blackman, "The Next Justices," *Weekly Standard*, September 14, 2015.

129   **"Ask this of potential court nominees"**: George Will, "The 110-Year-Old Case That Still Inspires Supreme Court Debates," *Washington Post*, July 10, 2015.

130   **"judicial tyranny"**: Emma Margolin, "Ted Cruz Goes After Supreme Court for 'Judicial Tyranny,'" MSNBC.com, July 22, 2015.

130   **"If we believe in judicial restraint"**: Senator Rand Paul, Comments on Judicial Restraint and Activism, Heritage Action Conservative Policy Summit, January 16, 2015, JoshBlackman .com.

130   **"I think he did it because he wanted"**: Jordyn Phelps, "Trump: Chief Justice Roberts Upheld Obamacare 'to Be Popular in the Beltway,'" ABCNews.com, December 12, 2015.

130   **a dubious constitutional principle**: James Uriah Blacksher and Lani Guinier, "Free at Last: Rejecting Equal Sovereignty and Restoring the Constitutional Right to Vote: Shelby County v. Holder," *Harvard Law and Policy Review* 8, no. 1 (2014).

131   **In *Citizens United*, too**: Sam Baker, "John Roberts: First Amendment Champion," *National Journal*, June 3, 2015.

Chapter 6: Pushing the Boundaries

133   **In 2011 Rob Natelson wrote a paper**: Robert G. Natelson, "Proposing Constitutional Amendments by Convention: Rules Governing the Process," *Tennessee Law Review* 78 (August 3, 2011): 693.

133   A low-key and self-effacing Montana-based: Rob Natelson, interview by author, c. September–October 2014.

133   "I just found a level of public interest": Ibid.

134   All of a sudden Natelson: Ibid.

134   ALEC asked him to produce: Robert G. Natelson, "Proposing Constitutional Amendments by a Convention of the States: A Handbook for State Lawmakers," prepared for the American Legislative Exchange Council.

134   At an Article V "symposium": Natelson at symposium, video posted on YouTube by Convention of States Project, April 23, 2014.

134   Even Harvard Law School held: Lewis Rice, "Tea Party and Liberals Convene at HLS to Discuss Constitutional Convention," Harvard Law School, October 5, 2011.

134   gathered at Mount Vernon: Emma Roller and David Weigel, "Give Me Amendments or Give Me Death," *Slate,* December 10, 2013.

134   one at the Indiana State Capitol: Dan Carden, "Indiana to Host Planning for State-Led Revisions to U.S. Constitution," *Northwest Indiana Times,* May 3, 2014.

134   one at the U.S. Naval Heritage Center: "Assembly of State Legislatures Meeting," C-SPAN, December 8, 2014.

134   As of January 2016, twenty-seven states: Michael Patrick Leahy, "How the Proposed 'Assembly of the States' Differs from an Article V Convention of the States," Breitbart.com, July 7, 2015.

134   They've been helped along by ALEC: "ALEC's Balanced Budget Amendment Policy," American Legislative Exchange Council.

134   Four red states: "Alabama Becomes Fourth State in History to Pass Convention of States Application," *PR Newswire,* May 22, 2015.

135   "put the prestige and power": David Weigel, "Rubio Endorses a New Constitutional Convention, Winning Praise from the Right," *Washington Post,* December 30, 2015.

135   Tom Coburn, the former Oklahoma senator: Tamara Colbert, "Tom Coburn Joins Convention of States Project as

Senior Adviser," press release, Convention of States Project, February 11, 2015.

135   **"a political inevitability":** Mark Meckler, "Bipartisan Committees Discuss Protocols for Inevitable Article V Convention," Breitbart.com, June 18, 2014.

135   **Randy Barnett, who's driving:** Randy E. Barnett, "The Case for a Federalism Amendment," *Wall Street Journal,* April 23, 2009.

135   **Tea Party senators write books:** Mike Lee, *Our Lost Constitution: The Willful Subversion of America's Founding Documents* (New York: Sentinel, 2015).

135   **The exercise ran into trouble:** Jennifer Steinhauer, "Constitution Has Its Day (More or Less) in House," *New York Times,* January 6, 2011.

136   **Other conservatives have been:** Alan Greenblatt, "Rethinking the 17th Amendment: An Old Idea Gets Fresh Opposition," NPR, February 5, 2014.

136   **to protect the Constitution's blatantly undemocratic**: Tara Ross, "The Electoral College Ensures All Voices Are Heard," *U.S. News and World Report,* November 5, 2012.

136   **to rig it even further:** Dana Leibelson, "The GOP's Plan to Rig the Electoral College, Explained," *Mother Jones,* January 31, 2013.

136   **throw a wrench in the system:** Charles Murray, *By the People: Rebuilding Liberty Without Permission* (New York: Crown Forum, 2015).

137   **"The United States is not in fact":** Charles Cooke, "Repeal the 17th Amendment!," *National Review,* March 1, 2013.

137   **Of course, proponents of Article V:** Natelson interview.

137   **a balanced budget amendment:** "27 States Eye Constitutional Amendment on Balanced Budget," Newsmax.com, April 6, 2015.

137   **stricter definition of the Commerce Clause:** Philip Klein, "Is It Time for a Convention?," *American Spectator,* October 2010.

137   **the Repeal Amendment:** Ibid.

137   **all three are included on a list:** Mark Levin, *The Liberty Amendments: Restoring the American Republic* (New York: Threshold, 2014).

137 **"return lawmaking"**: Lana Shadwick, "Texas Governor Calls for Article V Constitutional Convention," Breitbart.com, January 8, 2016.

138 **By President George W. Bush's second term**: Bob Bernick Jr., "Legislators Seek Say over U.S. Senators," *Deseret News*, January 24, 2006.

138 **So in 2006 Stephenson introduced**: Bernick, "Legislators Seek Say."

139 **All of a sudden, during that campaign**: Felicia Sonmez, "The 17th Amendment Resurfaces as a Campaign Issue," *Washington Post*, October 11, 2010.

139 **In Congress, Representative Louie Gohmert**: Eric Kleefeld, "Gohmert: Fight Health Care Bill by Repealing Popular Election of Senators," *Talking Points Memo*, March 23, 2010.

139 **Rick Perry came out against**: Ian Millhiser, "Rick Perry Calls Two Constitutional Amendments 'Mistaken,'" *Think Progress*, November 2, 2010.

139 **"the decline of so-called states' rights"**: Quoted in Ian Millhiser, "Scalia Jumps on the Anti-Seventeenth Amendment Bandwagon," *Think Progress*, November 15, 2010.

139 **"constitutional conservative"**: David Catanese, "Sen. Bennett Loses GOP Nomination," *Politico*, May 8, 2010. On Lee as a Seventeenth Amendment repeal supporter, see Greenblatt, "Rethinking the 17th Amendment."

139 **After Obama's 2012 reelection**: M. Alex Johnson, "Democrats Make Gains in Senate Majority," NBCNews.com, November 6, 2012.

139 **"If you have the ability to hire and fire me"**: Quoted in Ian Millhiser, "Ted Cruz Suggests His Own Election to the Senate Should Be Unconstitutional," *Think Progress*, December 6, 2013.

139 **"not germane to ALEC's mission"**: Amanda Terkel, "ALEC Drops Proposed Legislation Chipping Away at the 17th Amendment," *Huffington Post*, January 23, 2014.

140 **"more coolness"**: Unless otherwise indicated, all quotes from the debate at the Constitutional Convention are from Madison's notes at Avalon Project, Yale Law School.

140 **"Senate should come from"**: Rufus King's notes on the debate

at the Constitutional Convention, May 31, 1787, Avalon Project, Yale Law School.

141 **"It is as difficult for a poor man":** Jay S. Bybee, "Ulysses at the Mast: Democracy, Federalism, and the Sirens' Song of the 17th Amendment," paper 350, *Scholarly Works, Northwestern University Law Review*, 1997.

141 **"He is a shame to the American nation":** Mark Twain, "Senator Clark of Montana," in *Mark Twain in Eruption: Hitherto Unpublished Pages About Men and Events*, ed. Bernard De Voto (New York: Harper, 1940)

141 **Six years later an exposé:** David Graham Philips, "The Treason of the Senate," *Cosmopolitan*, February 1906.

141 **"What has the Senate done":** Ibid.

142 **"I think that it is best":** *Papers Relating to the Election of Senators by Direct Vote of the People* (Washington, D.C.: U.S. Government Printing Office, 1908), p. 28.

142 **"a separate branch of Congress":** Quoted in Ralph A. Rossum, *Federalism, the Supreme Court, and the Seventeenth Amendment* (New York: Lexington Books, 2001), p. 118.

142 **Led by lawmakers from western states:** Bybee, "Ulysses at the Mast."

143 **All this came on top of a raft:** Ronald J. Pestritto, "Woodrow Wilson: Godfather of Liberalism," Heritage Foundation, July 31, 2012.

143 **a historic villain:** David Greenberg, "Hating Woodrow Wilson," *Slate*, October 22, 2010.

143 **"crisis in Constitutionalism":** All quotations in this paragraph and the next are from Michael Kammen, *A Machine That Would Go of Itself: The Constitution in American Culture* (Piscataway, N.J.: Transaction, 2006), pp. 206, 220–33 passim.

145 **"For at least since the time of the Greeks":** Robert Welch, "The Truth in Time," *American Opinion*, November 1, 1966.

146 **"serious deterioration in states rights":** Quoted in Tim Murphy, "How W. Cleon Skousen Whitewashed American History," *Mother Jones*, April 2010.

146 **"extravagant spending":** Zell Miller, Floor Statement on Repealing the 17th Amendment, April 28, 2004.

146 **"Senators were originally chosen by the state legislatures":** "2004 Third IL Senate Debate: on Government Reform," OnTheIssues.org, October 21, 2004.

147 **Instead, electors soon began:** "Who Are the Electors?," National Archives and Records Administration.

147 **Since almost all states:** "Problems with the Electoral College," FairVote.org.

147 **Then factor in that the allocation:** "Distribution of Electoral Votes," National Archives and Records Administration.

148 **odd system has handed:** D'Angelo Gore, "Presidents Winning Without Popular Vote," FactCheck.org, March 24, 2008.

148 **the system encourages:** "Problems with the Electoral College," FairVote.org.

148 **the electors are even today:** "Faithless Electors," FairVote.org. In 2004 one West Virginia Republican elector threatened during the fall presidential campaign to become such a "faithless elector" by giving his vote to John Kerry, not George W. Bush. Doing so would have thrown the contest into turmoil if the candidates had finished tied in the Electoral College, as looked possible at the time. (He stuck with Bush in the end.)

148 **"indefensible":** Sanford Levinson and John McGinnis, "Debate: Should We Dispense with the Electoral College?," *University of Pennsylvania Law Review* 155 (2007).

148 **The National Popular Vote (NPV) campaign:** "Explanation of National Popular Vote Bill," National Popular Vote campaign.

148 **"Here's a way that we can elect":** "Hendrik Hertzberg of *The New Yorker*: Reform the Presidential Election System to Promote Greater Civic Health," Shorenstein Center on Media, Politics and Public Policy, Harvard Kennedy School, September 16, 2014.

149 **"Our system for electing a president":** Bradley A. Smith, "Vanity of Vanities: National Popular Vote and the Electoral College," *Election Law Journal: Rules, Politics, and Policy* 7, no. 3 (2008): 196–217.

149 **That's the view of Tara Ross:** Tara Ross, *Enlightened Democracy: The Case for the Electoral College* (Miami: Colonial Press, 2004). See Ross's bio at TaraRoss.com.

149   **The Heritage Foundation, too:** Hans A. von Spakovsky, "Destroying the Electoral College: The Anti-Federalist National Popular Vote Scheme," Heritage Foundation, October 27, 2011.

150   **"we could see the end of presidential candidates":** "Do You Understand the Electoral College?" and "The Popular vote vs. the Electoral College," videos posted on the website of Prager University, May 17, 2015.

150   **"The Founders had no intention":** Ibid.

150   **Not a single state:** "61% of the Way to Activating the National Popular Vote Bill," National Popular Vote campaign.

150   **Currently, every state except Maine:** "Maine and Nebraska," FairVote.org.

151   **But Republican state lawmakers:** Brendan Fischer, "GOP Vote Rigging Stalls in Virginia and Florida but Pushes On in Wisconsin and Michigan–Why?," *PRWatch,* January 28, 2013.

151   **One relatively typical version:** Ian Millhiser, "GOP Pennsylvania Gov. Tom Corbett Proposes Rigging the Electoral College for Republicans," *Think Progress,* September 14, 2011.

151   **If that had been done:** Ian Millhiser, "Top Pennsylvania GOP Lawmaker Proposes New Election Rigging Scheme," *Think Progress,* December 4, 2012.

151   **Charles Carrico, a Virginia state senator:** David Sherfinski, "Ohio, Virginia, Eye Proposals for More Proportional Split of Electoral Votes," *Washington Times,* December 8, 2012.

151   **"Michigan, which awards by popular vote":** Quoted in Jonathan Oosting, "Michigan Panel Debates Changes to Presidential Election System, Electoral College Vote," MLive.com, September 24, 2015.

151   **"ought to be looking at":** Patrick Marley, "Reince Priebus Backs Electoral Vote Change, but It's State's Decision," *Milwaukee Journal-Sentinel,* January 13, 2013.

152   **The election of Democratic governors:** Trip Gabriel, "Terry McAuliffe, Democrat, Is Elected Governor in Tight Race," *New York Times,* November 5, 2013; Zachary Warmbrodt, "Wolf · Ousts Gov. Corbett in Pa.," *Politico,* November 4, 2014.

152   **It wasn't long ago that Virginia:** Virginia gave its votes to the Republican in every presidential election from 1968 to 2004. See "Virginia Presidential Election Voting history," 270towin.com.

152   **A scholar at the American Enterprise Institute:** Richard J. Herrnstein and Charles Murray, *The Bell Curve: Intelligence and Class Structure in American Life* (New York: Free Press, 1994).

152   **But Murray's *Losing Ground*:** Charles Murray, *Losing Ground: American Social Policy, 1950–1980* (New York: Basic Books, 1984).

152   **Not long ago, when Jeb Bush:** Daniel Strauss, "Can't Unring That Bell: Jeb Bush Says He's a Fan of Charles Murray's Books," *Talking Points Memo,* April 30, 2015.

152   **Rand Paul and Paul Ryan:** Steve Benen, "A Controversial Author Finds a Powerful Audience," MSNBC.com, May 7, 2015.

152   **In his latest book:** Quotations from Charles Murray in this and the next three paragraphs are from his book *By the People: Reclaiming Liberty Without Permission* (New York: Crown Forum, 2015), pp. 104–5, 111, 115, 144–46.

154   **"Isn't it . . . a sort of sign":** "Rebuilding Liberty Without Permission: A Conversation with Charles Murray," American Enterprise Institute, May 14, 2015.

155   **"We are at the end of the American project":** Murray, *By the People,* p. xiii.

Chapter 7: Joining the Battle

157   **the plaintiff in an ambitious lawsuit:** *Griffin v. Branstad,* Iowa District Court for Polk County, complaint filed November 7, 2014.

157   **The suit was part of:** Christopher Uggen, Sarah Shannon, and Jeff Manza, "State-Level Estimates of Felon Disenfranchisement in the United States, 2010," Sentencing Project, July 2012.

157   **Griffin, a shy stay-at-home mom:** Kelli Griffin, interview by author for MSNBC, Des Moines, Iowa, January 22, 2015.

157   **Griffin had been through:** *Griffin v. Branstad* complaint.

158   **"I felt good":** Griffin interview.

158   **But not long after voting:** Ibid.

158   **A few months later Griffin:** *Griffin v. Branstad* complaint.

158   **she was looking at up to fifteen years:** Megan McNeill, "Jury Finds Griffin Not Guilty," *Daily Gate City,* March 21, 2014.

158   **two-year investigation into voter fraud:** *Griffin v. Branstad* complaint.

158   **voter ID law:** Jason Noble, "Secretary of State Matt Schultz Introduces Voter ID Bill, but Legislative Response Is Muted," *Des Moines Register,* January 26, 2012.

158   **the Iowa chair of Ted Cruz's presidential campaign:** Craig Robinson, "Cruz Names Iowa Leadership Team," *Iowa Republican,* April 30, 2015.

158   **a press release touting the charges:** Kevin Hall, "Charges Filed in Nine More Potential Voter Fraud Cases," *Iowa Republican,* January 22, 2014.

158   **When she began her probation:** *Griffin v. Branstad* complaint.

158   **in 2005 then-governor Tom Vilsack:** Ibid.

158   **on his very first day in office:** According to the "About the Governor" website, Branstad was "sworn into office on January 14, 2011." See also *Griffin v. Branstad:* "On January 14, 2011, the Governor signed Executive Order Number 70."

159   **Five years later:** E-mail to author from Colin Smith, deputy legal counsel to Governor Branstad, January 19, 2016.

159   **At her trial, Griffin testified:** *Griffin v. Branstad* complaint.

159   **"I was happy that I wasn't going":** Griffin interview.

159   **Still, fighting the charges:** Ibid.

159   **It aims to end once and for all:** *Griffin v. Branstad* complaint.

159   **around twenty thousand Iowans:** Rita Bettis, legal director, ACLU of Iowa, to author, January 4, 2016.

159   **Felon disenfranchisement laws:** "Felony Disenfranchisement: A Primer," policy brief, Sentencing Project.

159   **In April 2016, Virginia governor Terry McAuliffe:** Olympia Meola, "McAuliffe to Speed Rights Restoration," *Richmond Times-Dispatch,* April 17, 2014.

159   **Maryland lawmakers had:** Rachel Bluth, "Activists and Ex-Felons Demonstrate to Override Gov. Hogan's Veto," *Baltimore Post-Examiner,* January 15, 2016.

160   **And while Kentucky and Minnesota:** David Weigel, "Kentucky's New Governor Reverses Executive Order That Restored Voting Rights for Felons," *Washington Post,* December 23, 2015; Abby Simons, "Move to Restore Felon Voting Rights Appears Stalled," *Minneapolis Star-Tribune,* April 23, 2015.

160   **popping up in other states:** Dave Hon, "Schaaf Files Bill to

Give Voting Rights Back to Felons," *St. Joseph News-Press,* January 14, 2016.

160 **"menace of Negro domination":** Brent Staples, "The Racist Origins of Felon Disenfranchisement," *New York Times,* November 18, 2014.

160 **grassroots efforts at reform in Florida:** Steve Rosenfeld, "How a New Initiative to Give Felons Voting Rights Could Upend Florida's Political Landscape," AlterNet.com, May 5, 2015. For statistics on felon disenfranchisement in Florida, see Uggen, Shannon, and Manza, "State-Level Estimates of Felon Disenfranchisement." See also Spencer Woodman, "Thanks to Republicans, Nearly a Quarter of Florida's Black Citizens Can't Vote," TheIntercept.com, December 9, 2015.

160 **The nascent shift on felon voting:** Russell Berman, "The Moment for Criminal Justice Reform?" TheAtlantic.com, July 10, 2015.

160 **"It's quite difficult from":** Julie Ebenstein, interview by author for MSNBC, January 16, 2015.

160 **an emerging movement:** J. Mijin Cha and Liz Kennedy, "Millions to the Polls," Demos, February 2014.

160 **increasing small-dollar campaign contributions:** Sundeep Iyer, Elisabeth Genn, Brendan Glavin, and Michael J. Malbin, "Donor Diversity Through Public Matching Funds," Brennan Center for Justice, May 14, 2012.

161 **voter ID laws in Pennsylvania, Missouri, and Arkansas:** Rick Lyman, "Pennsylvania Voter ID Law Struck Down as Judge Cites Burden on Citizens," *New York Times,* January 17, 2014; "Missouri: Voter ID Law Is Struck Down," Associated Press, September 15, 2006; Emma G. Fitzsimmons, "Arkansas Supreme Court Strikes Down Voter ID Law, Saying It Exceeds State Constitution," *New York Times,* October 15, 2014.

161 **In Ohio, some weekend voting:** Robert Higgs, "ACLU, Secretary of State Jon Husted Settle Federal Lawsuit over Access to Early Voting in Ohio," *Cleveland Plain-Dealer,* April 17, 2015.

161 **North Carolina's draconian:** Anne Blythe and Colin Campbell, "N.C. Legislature Votes to Soften Voter ID Requirement," *News and Observer,* June 18, 2015.

162   **"If everybody voted":** Jesse Byrnes, "President Obama Floats Mandatory Voting," *Hill,* March 19, 2015.

162   **Voter Expansion Project:** Frank James, "Clintons Provide Firepower Behind DNC 'Voter Expansion Project,'" NPR, February 27, 2014.

162   **In just the first four and a half months:** "Voting Laws Roundup 2015," Brennan Center for Justice, June 3, 2015.

162   **"We've seen increasing momentum":** Quoted in Zachary Roth, "In 2015, Hope and Fear on Voting Rights," MSNBC .com, December 29, 2015.

162   **Those who study voting:** Steven Carbo, "Benefits of Same Day Registration," Demos, January 9, 2012.

163   **And so in 2015 Oregon:** Jeff Guo, "It's Official: New Oregon Law Will Automatically Register People to Vote," *Washington Post,* March 17, 2015.

163   **Several months later California:** Brakkton Booker, "California Becomes 2nd State to Automatically Register Voters," NPR, October 11, 2015.

163   **As of November 2015, legislators:** "Automatic Voter Registration," Brennan Center for Justice, December 1, 2015.

163   **"would have a profound impact":** Evan Halper, "Hillary Clinton Attacks Republicans over Voting Restrictions," *Los Angeles Times,* June 4, 2015.

163   **Two months later her top rival:** S-1970—Raising Enrollment with a Government Initiated System for Timely Electoral Registration (REGISTER) Act of 2015, introduced August 5, 2015.

163   **New Jersey's bill passed:** Samantha Lachman, "Chris Christie Vetoes Election Reform Bill in New Jersey," *Huffington Post,* November 9, 2015.

164   **the two have sparred:** Zachary Roth, "Clinton, Sanders Vie as Voting Rights Champions," MSNBC.com, November 7, 2015.

164   **Since 2013 Takoma Park and Hyattsville:** Arelis R. Hernandez, "Hyattsville Becomes Second U.S. Municipality to Lower Voting Age to 16," *Washington Post,* January 14, 2015.

164   **twice the rate of everyone else:** Patrick Madden, "Unlikely Advocates Push to Give 16-Year-Olds a Vote—and a Voice," NPR, January 18, 2016.

164   **San Francisco is exploring:** Emily Green, "Plan to Allow S.F.

16-Year-Olds to Vote Won't Be on 2015 Ballot," *San Francisco Chronicle*, June 8, 2015.

164   **a proposal in Washington, D.C.:** Joe Helm, "D.C.'s 16- and 17-Year-Olds Are Eager to Vote for President. But Should They?," *Washington Post*, November 13, 2015.

164   **Brazil, Austria, Argentina, and some states in Germany:** Mike MacNevin, "Millions of 16- and 17-Year-Olds Vote in Brazilian Presidential Election, but No President Elected," FairVote.org, October 23, 2014.

164   **Twelve U.S. states allow:** Michelle Manchir, "Youth Vote Gets Younger: Law Lets Most 17-Year-Olds Cast Ballot," *Chicago Tribune*, March 3, 2014.

164   **And indeed, a growing body:** "Lower the Voting Age," FairVote.org.

164   **"mid-adolescents":** Vivian E. Hamilton, "Democratic Inclusion, Cognitive Development, and the Age of Electoral Majority," *Brooklyn Law Review*, Summer 2012.

165   **New York City recently considered:** Matthew Chayes, "NYC Council to Decide on Letting Noncitizens Vote in Local Elections," *Newsday*, March 2, 2015.

165   **In 1848 Wisconsin, whose population:** Alexander Keyssar, *The Right to Vote: The Contested History of Democracy in the United States* (New York: Basic Books, 2000), p. 33.

165   **"upright, honorable, and industrious":** Ibid., p. 83.

165   **"Enfranchising non-citizens would make":** Kanishk Tharoor, "Non-citizens in New York City Could Soon Be Given the Right to Vote," *Guardian*, April 2, 2015.

165   **When President Obama mused:** Byrnes, "Obama Floats Mandatory Voting."

165   **feverish conservative nightmares:** J. Christian Adams, "Decoding Obama's Mandatory Voting Fantasy," *PJ Media*, March 23, 2015; Josh Feldman, "Fox Pundits Outraged by Obama's Mandatory Voting Comments, While Rupert Murdoch Agrees," *Mediaite*, March 19, 2015.

165   **Australia, Belgium, and Brazil:** Laura Santhanam, "22 Countries Where Voting Is Mandatory," PBS.org, November 3, 2014.

166   **As you'd expect, studies show:** Dr. Lisa Hill and Jonathan

Louth, "Compulsory Voting Laws and Turnout: Efficacy and Appropriateness," paper presented to the Australasian Political Studies Association Conference, University of Adelaide, September–October 2004.

166   **Nicholas Stephanopoulos, a law professor:** Nicholas Stephanopoulos, "A Feasible Roadmap to Compulsory Voting," The Atlantic.com, November 2, 2015.

166   **"The power of using local law":** Josh Douglas, "Should 16- and 17-Year-Olds Be Allowed to Vote?," PrawfsBlawg, November 13, 2015.

167   **The state's Hispanic population:** Corrie MacLaggan, "Report: Texas Lags in Hispanic Voter Turnout," *Texas Tribune,* February 26, 2014.

167   **Battleground Texas:** Zachary Roth, "Battleground Texas: Inside the Fight to Turn the State Blue," MSNBC.com, May 2, 2014.

168   **field campaign for Wendy Davis:** Christopher Hooks, "Losing Ground," *Texas Observer,* December 30, 2014.

169   **fight back against gerrymandering:** Rebecca Beitsch, "Amid Court Fights, Some States Consider Redistricting Commissions," Pew Charitable Trusts, September 23, 2015.

169   **There's not enough evidence:** Ibid.; Sam Wang, "The Great Gerrymander of 2012," *New York Times,* February 2, 2013.

169   **These efforts got a boost:** Adam Liptak, "Supreme Court Rebuffs Lawmakers over Independent Redistricting Panel," *New York Times,* June 29, 2015.

169   **"drawing our congressional districts":** Javier Panzar, "Obama's State of the Union Pledge to Push for Bipartisan Redistricting Reform Was a Late Add," *Los Angeles Times,* January 13, 2016.

169   **backing from Clinton, Sanders:** Paul Blumenthal, "Hillary Clinton Releases Broad Campaign Finance Reform Plan," *Huffington Post,* September 8, 2015; Justin Miller, "Bernie Knows Repealing Citizens United Isn't Enough. Does Anyone Else?," *American Prospect,* August 7, 2015; Cameron Joseph, "Dems Want Campaign Finance Constitutional Amendment," *Hill,* July 15, 2014.

169   **New York City gives candidates:** Alec MacGillis, "Wall Street

Isn't Shaping the New York Mayoral Race. Thank Public Financing," *New Republic,* September 2, 2013.

170   **a program that gives every voter four:** Russell Berman, "Seattle's Experiment with Campaign Funding," TheAtlantic.com, November 10, 2015.

170   **"would provoke tens of millions":** Bruce Ackerman and Ian Ayres, "Democracy Dollars Can Give Every Voter a Real Voice in American Politics," *Washington Post,* November 5, 2015.

170   **"anticorruption box":** Richard L. Hasen, Plutocrats United: *Campaign Money, the Supreme Court and the Distortion of American Elections* (New Haven: Yale University Press, 2016).

170   **"The principle of equality governs":** Lee Drutman, "Enough About Our 'Corrupt Campaign Finance System' Already. Let's Talk Equality," Vox, February 5, 2016.

171   **an across-the-board hard-right shift:** Ian Millhiser, "How One Multi-Millionaire Is Turning North Carolina into a Tea Party Utopia," *Think Progress,* April 8, 2013.

171   **In 2013 alone North Carolina:** Zachary Roth, "In North Carolina, a Hard-Right Shift Hits a Roadblock," MSNBC.com, November 29, 2013.

171   **In doing so, it pushed people:** Ibid.

172   **Pat McCrory, who faces:** Tom Jensen, "McCrory Approval Hits New Low," Public Policy Polling, July 9, 2015; Jensen, "McCrory Continues to Struggle; Burr Leads Dem Field by 7–8," Public Policy Polling, August 20, 2015.

172   **it's spawned offshoots:** Sophia Tesfaye, "Cornel West, Deray McKesson Arrested During 'Moral Mondays' Protest in Ferguson," *Salon,* August 10, 2015.

173   **a $25 million political organization:** Ken Thomas, "Clinton Allies Forming Group to Protect, Register Voters," Associated Press, February 10, 2016.

Epilogue

175   **Snyder admitted in a major speech:** Rick Snyder, State of the State address, January 19, 2016.

175   **The poisoned water had been linked:** "Flint Hospital Suspected

River, Legionnaire's Disease Link," CBS/Associated Press, January 23, 2016.

175 **"No citizen of this great state":** Snyder, State of the State address, January 19, 2016.

176 **empowered state-appointed "emergency managers":** Michigan Radio Newsroom, "Seven Things to Know About Michigan's Emergency Manager Law," Michigan Radio, December 6, 2011.

176 **a right-wing, Koch-funded Michigan think tank:** Louis Schimmel Jr., "Can Detroit's Problems Be Corrected by an Emergency Financial Manager?," Mackinac Center for Public Policy, December 5, 2005.

176 **Snyder would soon appoint:** Paul Abowd, "Michigan's Hostile Takeover," *Mother Jones,* February 15, 2012.

176 **saw the law as a patronizing rebuke:** Chris Lewis, "Does Michigan's Emergency-Manager Law Disenfranchise Black Citizens?," *Atlantic,* May 9, 2013.

176 **In one city, Benton Harbor:** Mark Brush, "Emergency Manager of Benton Harbor Strips Power from Elected Officials," Michigan Radio, April 16, 2011.

176 **In 2012 opponents collected:** Jonathan Oosting, "Michigan Proposal 1: Voters Reject Measure, Repeal Controversial Emergency Manager Law," Michigan Live, November 7, 2012.

176 **the wrong font size:** Abowd, "Michigan's Hostile Takeover."

176 **decisively approved the law's repeal:** Oosting, "Michigan Proposal 1."

177 **a new emergency manager law:** John Conyers, "Flint Is the Predicted Outcome of Michigan's Long, Dangerous History with Emergency Managers," *Nation,* February 17, 2016.

177 **four different emergency managers:** Ron Fonger, "Ex-Emergency Manager Says He's Not to Blame for Flint River Water Switch," MLive.com, October 27, 2015.

177 **undertaken to save money:** Ron Fonger, "Flint Water Problems: Switch Aimed to Save $5 Million—but at What Cost?," MLive.com, January 23, 2015.

177 **under dispute:** Fonger, "Ex-emergency Manager Says He's Not to Blame."

177   **failed to respond forcefully to complaints:** "How Flint Water Crisis Emerged," MLive.com, October 2015.

177   **rejected an offer to reconnect Flint:** Findings of Michigan auditor general in letter to Senate Minority Leader Jim Ananich, December 23, 2015.

177   **"State officials, in fact":** Richard Schragger, "Flint Wasn't Allowed Democracy," *Slate,* February 8, 2016.

177   **in January 2015, Snyder removed Earley:** Julie Bosman, "Flint's Former Manager Resigns as Head of Detroit Schools," *New York Times,* February 2, 2016.

178   **had ended, remarkably, in a tie:** Richard Fausset and Alan Blinder, "Republicans Unseat Mississippi Democrat Who Drew Winning Straw After Race Ended in Tie," *New York Times,* January 20, 2016.

178   **a major new corporate tax cut:** Richard Fausset, "Mississippi Republicans Face Hard Tax Cut Choices," *New York Times,* January 21, 2016.

178   **"state-mandated wage suppression":** Teresa Tritch, "The Backlash in Birmingham," *New York Times,* February 29, 2016.

179   **nullifying the Charlotte law:** Dave Philipps, "North Carolina Bans Local Anti-Discrimination Policies," *New York Times,* March 23, 2016.

179   **"super-preemption" bill:** Jim Nintzel, "The Skinny," *Tucson Weekly,* March 24, 2016.

179   **Scott Walker:** Zachary Roth, "Wisconsin Throws Up Major Voter Registration Hurdle," MSNBC.com, March 25, 2016.

179   **"most unfortunate mistakes":** Emily Larson, "Legislature Passes Resolution Calling for Repeal of 17th Amendment," *Deseret News,* March 2, 2016.

180   **The protest, known as Democracy Spring:** Democracyspring .org.

180   **a broad-based "attack on democracy":** "Democracy at a Crossroads: How the One Percent Is Silencing Our Voices," Democracy Initiative Education Fund.

Index

About the Author

ZACHARY ROTH is a national reporter for MSNBC. He was born and raised in London, and lives with his family in Brooklyn.